Armando Oscar Cavanha Filho

USERCHAIN
End User Logistics
topics for discussion

Second Edition

Editor and Publisher: Armando Oscar Cavanha Filho
Cover Design: Rodrigo de Campos Cavanha
Translation: Tânia Gastão Saliés

This book shows some Brazilian references and recommends readings in Portuguese because its original was written and published in Brazil.

USERCHAIN: End User Logistics – topics for discussion

ISBN: 978-0-9791930-2-6

cavanha.com
cavanha.net
userchain.com
userchain.net

Houston, TX, USA - 2008

SUMMARY

To
Ricardo de Campos Cavanha
Rodrigo de Campos Cavanha
Victor Gribel Cavanha

"Be certain of your doubts."
Saint Thomas Aquinas
Saint Thomas of Aquin
Saint Thomas Aquino
São Tomás de Aquino

FOREWORD

It gives me great pleasure to write the foreword to this edition of the book Logistics Strategies – topics for discussion – by Armando Oscar Cavanha Filho. Indeed, Logistics is an art, the art of managing and controlling the flow of materials, goods, services, energy and so on and so forth, from the source of production to the marketplace. In the modern world, particularly in the oil & gas industry, it is almost impossible to accomplish any marketing, manufacturing, developing, refining, and distribution of petroleum products without logistics support. It is indeed a critical success factor. Generally speaking, it comprehends the integration of information, transportation, inventory, warehousing, material handling, and packaging, in a complex and large spectrum of activities that require intelligent processes so as to achieve safe and timely delivery, at the lowest possible cost.

In this respect, Armando Cavanha, who has a distinguished career in the petroleum industry, particularly in leading the activities of procurement at Petrobras, was very successful on synthesizing his large experience in this book, which is an excellent overview of concepts and techniques covering complex subjects, with accessible and didactic language. The book also provides a valuable contribution to those who are keen to learn or update their knowledge of logistics strategies by advancing a relevant selection of readings.

I remember an outstanding presentation by Armando Cavanha, held at the British Chamber for Commerce and Industry in Brazil, in Rio de Janeiro, back on June 8th., 2005. At that opportunity, he shared his views of procurement for oil & gas development projects at Petrobras with the audience. Some of the points he addressed at that occasion can also be seen in this book; mostly, they regard the process of procurement and Logistics that have supported Petrobras to develop large deepwater oil fields in Brazil successfully.

I also would like to seize the opportunity to highlight Armando Cavanha's ability to advise colleagues on matters which are Logistics-related. In this respect, I would like to express my profound thanks for the great help he provided me with, when I was invited by INTSOK, an oil and gas industry and Norwegian government-supported organization, to speak about Petrobras growing upstream portfolio and the oil & gas supply and service industry, at the INTSOK International Oil & Gas Business Day, held in Stavanger, on August 23rd ,2004.

Finally, Petrobras' ever growing activities in Brazil and international contexts, its recent-reached status as an investment grade company, its presence in the Dow Jones index, and its second position in the ranking published by Spain's Management & Excellence—a measure of oil companies' performance in corporate governance, transparency, ethics, socio-environmental responsibility and sustainability—attest the great contribution Armando Cavanha and his team have provided the Company with. The procurement process, which includes vendors' transparency programmes, has been one the parameters of each of these instances of Petrobras' success.

Houston, April 4th 2007

João C. A. Figueira
Senior Vice President – Upstream
Petrobras America, Inc.

Introduction

This book brings to light various Logistics-related topics within the scope of my professional experience. Its objective is to allow you to construe a complementary understanding of the main movements in Logistics, a topic so broad, complex and up to date. In doing so, it does not commit itself to any classic, methodological or sequential approaches, but to collecting ideas and issues that should be debated and adapted case by case, according to the logistics of each specific business or type of logistics support.

Actually, my goal in writing it was to discuss the strategic reasoning behind logistics for production. For that purpose, I present concepts such as standardization, regionalization, supplier differenced treatments, alliances, partnerships, contingency, and USERCHAIN. I also discuss several issues such as reasons for new business approaches and how to reach sustained productive processes.

The reasons for new business approaches in productive activities have a competitive foundation: Business survival. Contemporary society has accelerated the differentiation between values, emphasized the capacity to establish different ways of understanding each asset, whether physical or intellectual. The current key expressions are "How much is it worth," "how much is it's worth perceived to be," each "thing" and each "time." It is the era of intangibles, in an imperfect synergy with tangible assets.

There is space for technological innovation, corporate mergers and alliances, while always focusing on the business directives, strategy, and profitability. Concepts that do not pay, that do not give a return on investments, in a short time, or that give large returns within longer terms, but with assured guarantee, are not sustainable. Ideas are put into practice and are left to their own fate in a hurried, virtualized world, which is not concerned about satisfying those who produce or conceive them, but about remunerating "for what is used," for the added value that is transmitted fleetingly.

Logistics is one of the business subjects that has academically deepened knowledge both in how to provide differential support to service and information productive chains, and in interfaces of distributed products for end clients. People who ask for and intend to use something also want to be certain that they will be "receiving that which they ordered," in the time, the quantity, the quality, and in the manner that they had configured it. Therefore, service is important, but communication about it and confidence in it are perhaps even more important than the service itself. There is no space for disappointing the clients. Future compensation is acceptable, however, uncertain. Everything has to be precise, exact, and with a dynamic reply.

The information offered at the time of the sale should be strictly complied with at the time of delivery, with traceability, price transparency, and guarantee of its contents. Logistics must not be forgotten in the marketing project, which needs to include the accessibility to the end client in its geographical areas of distribution. In other words, this is the era of confidence, where the supplier has to be just one "click" away and at a minimum distance from the consumer. To promise is to comply with, during the complete life cycle of goods and services offered. Post-sale and post-use competences are marks of recognition. Environmental issues, Reverse Logistics, e-solutions, the cost of shortages and so many other new standards determined by consumption have given birth to organizations as well as signed their death sentences, in just a blink of an eye.

Given the power of those who use products, judge and decide about who should or not be in the supplier market, it remains to be seen if the next steps in Logistics will be even more differentiated than current ones, even more determinant of organizations' existence.

Therefore, this book specially focuses on supply and service strategies in Logistics, a field that does not limit itself to analyzing frequent daily transactional activities. Although there are conceptual similarities between logistics for external clients as compared to logistics for internal clients (partners with the same end objective) or production, these two Logistics have separate characteristics.

The first, which involves processes related to the business marketing and image, has particularities relative to the clients who pay, to the interface market between separate companies or entities. It entails competitors in the same client market, anticipations, and sales.

The second, which aims at internal clients or partners, focuses on the internal productive process, on the supply of resources for an efficient production without any shortages. It takes a collaborative/cooperative viewpoint in which both suppliers and internal clients share the same objectives. They are partners. Furthermore, if either of them are not efficient or do not reach an objective, both (the supplier and the internal client) lose, which would not happen with traditional clients and suppliers (external), each one in a company (or side) and with separate objectives.

The vision of the complete chain, the arrangement between upstream and downstream activities and the control of related logistics interfaces form the basis for deeper studies with indicators, standards, descriptions of activities, relations between productive processes, and support. Such a vision amounts to a complete and comprehensive management necessary to reach sustained productive processes.

Without a clear direction and strategy, Logistics becomes no more than a set of sheer technical backup forces, not always aligned in the same direction and purpose, neither converging to the same result.

Within a broader view of Logistics, Support Logistics has different limits. Some include procurement in it, others do not. In reality, these concepts are flexible within this broader view. There is no right or wrong answer, but separate study approaches.

These are some of the issues this book highlights and that I would like to share with you.

Armando Oscar Cavanha Filho
Houston,
Jun/2008

1 –Logistics

Various worldwide organizations have tried to define and conceptualize Logistics in different ways. There is a true competition among them to adhere to updated perceptions of the term throughout time. Logistics, Supply Chain, User Chain, Demand Chain, including and excluding procurement and purchasing, warehousing, information systems are terms that represent the search for methodologies that maximize the comprehension and generation of perfect representative equations for the movement and physical availability of items in production or sales.

The concepts of Logistics and productive chain are distinct. The differentiating factor rests on the product cycle of each one of them. As a function of the type of company, defined by its most marked characteristics, there are different types of productive chains and logistics cycles. For example, the products of each productive chain of a soft drink manufacturer are the soft drinks themselves, functions of the different types demanded by the market, at a cost which allows competition and determined rates of return on investment, with the characteristics defined by marketing and quality assured by production and inputs.

On the other hand, the product of the Logistics Chain of this very same company may be considered as the perfect integration among the purchase of raw materials and inputs, their adequate availability for production, withdrawal from production, and distribution to the market, in time and to the right place, with controlled costs and information.

These concepts are not final and are open for discussion in academic and business environments. There are areas of overlap between Production and Logistics, as between Logistics and Marketing, as well as various other so-called fuzzy areas among disciplines. They are interfaces with differentiated knowledge and coverage, mainly in companies said to be complex (multiple functions, multiple products), depending on the organizational and management models they adopt.

In general, companies may be classified into three different types, according to their main characteristics. Namely:

- Technological
- Transformation / Production
- Logistics

This doesn't mean that each type of organization holds only a single Logistics characteristic, but that such characteristic is more evident and dominant in each one, differentiating and classifying each into a group type. Figure 1 shows, schematically, the differentiation between the three distinct types of companies.

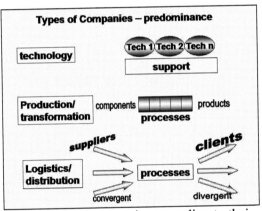

Figure 1 - Types of companies according to their main characteristics

Companies with a Technological predominance emphasize technological processes in their productive chain, having Logistics as a support, a complement, since the main value is substantially added by the differential system of techniques which are employed in their production. Normally characterized by a strong technical body and high investments in technological or scientific research, they must be intensely up to date and have a perfect sense of opportunity for the expansion of knowledge from a worldwide point of view.

Companies where production / transformation predominates already provide greater breadth for the logistics process when compared to the previous ones. They try to balance Production and Logistics. A shortage in one of the activities unbalances the system and leads to possible market losses. The focus on production/transformation becomes more intense in the manufacturing processes, in the techniques and management of product transformation plants, as well as in the qualification of inputs, processes, and physical products.

Companies with a Logistics / Distribution predominance, on their part, strongly rely on Logistics concepts. Their very essence is the correct treatment of flows and movements. Although such a treatment of the topic is not novel— since the times of military invasions, wars, and dominions the topic has been contemplated by various studies— Logistics has been rapidly transforming and adapting itself to current needs. Today, it plays an important role in management sciences, even with its limitations and difficult to define interfaces.

The differentiation between the logistics flow and productive chain of a system is vitally important. It avoids the extension of each domain and coverage and eliminates risks of deforming the concepts and reducing business efficiency.

For the purposes of this work, logistics flow and its associated costs are constituted by the following component stages:

- Acquisition of prime materials;
- Contracting of infrastructure services, production support, and physical movement;
- Transportation of raw materials to the warehouses;
- Physical distribution to the Distribution Centers;
- Transportation and delivery of finished products to the clients;
- Financial costs of stock (PRODUCT);
- Cost of not selling (because of product shortages in production or in the market) or Cost of shortages.

In a company's productive process, input logistics relates to the materials for production, while output logistics relates to the movement of the finished products to the market. Both situations involve an analysis of the demands and definition of the quantities, manners of transportation, that is, all the logistics issues previously mentioned.

Figure 2 illustrates the logistics flow in a typical production/transformation company by means of a generic diagram. It shows three levels of movement in the system: The physical (materials, products), financial (money), and information flows. The three flows go in both directions, that is, upstream and downstream, and vice-versa.

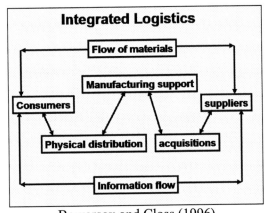

Bowersox and Closs (1996)
Figure 2 – Integrated Logistics

Figure 3 presents the three flows mentioned earlier, at a greater level of detail, explaining some functions/documents of the process and illustrating the cycle from the raw materials to the sale of the end product up to the consumer market. By showing Figure 3, I aim at characterizing the contours of the reasoning behind it, espoused by classic concepts that were advanced by renowned authors (Christopher, 1992; Bowersox & Closs, 1996; Blanchard, 1992). That is, even with the advances in technology and new approaches, some authors keep alive the characterization of the dimensions in Logistics as a continuum.

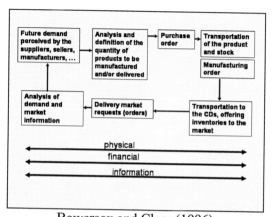

Bowersox and Closs (1996)
Figure 3 – The Three Flows in Logistics

The concept of Logistics leads to a view of the complete chain in the process of supplying materials, going from the activities at the start of the logistics flow until the activities considered final.

Figure 4 presents a schematic flow of the process of materials supply, its varied stages, and the associated cost of each sub-process individually, and in an accumulated way.

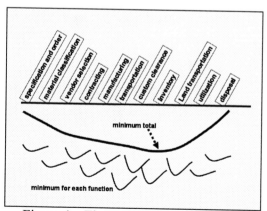

Figure 4 – The Materials Supply Cycle

The acquisition cycle starts in the specification of the demand for use and goes through various stages, reaching the application and disposal. Each stage has its times, risks, and costs, and they co-exist. This coexistence yields a sum total of cost for the stages and configures a region of minimal total cost. Each curve of each activity has a point of minimum cost and the sum total of the costs of all the activities produces a graph that has a general minimum cost for each environmental situation. It is reasonable to believe that the minimum cost for each activity *per se* is not what people look for, but the sum of the costs for the organization, given an expected level of service.

The Logistics Chain may be seen in Figure 5. Porter (1990) has divided the productive cycle of a generic company in productive chain and general functions, like procurement (Purchase of parts and services), which permeates the whole productive chain. The limits between Acquisition and inbound and outbound Logistics are fundamental for good business results, which brings to light the need for good management of interfaces.

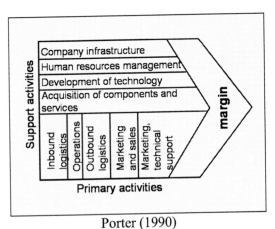

Porter (1990)

Figure 5 – The Productive Cycle of a Generic Company

The concept of Supply Chain involves not only the internal players of the corporation but also suppliers and clients, which increases the value of the chain under analysis.

Once the scope of logistics relationships moves outside the boundaries of the company, more resources and greater managerial sophistication are required.

Pecht (1995), when addressing Logistics support, brings up the theme "shortage" by approaching supply reliability within a complex system where usage reliability, maintenance, working life, and supplies interact. Based on this understanding, we may say that the reliability of a system relates to the complete cycle of its associated areas, from engineering, to maintenance, to Logistics. Any failure at one point in the cycle causes a failure of the whole cycle itself.

For example, in asset intensive industries, where investments and durable goods are relevant, Logistics flows may occur differently, with greater or less separation between upstream and downstream productive chains, with distinct logistics consequences. This means that for each business there is an appropriate organization and Logistics. To exemplify the concept of logistics flows, Figure 6 shows "upstream" and "downstream" actions in the oil industry.

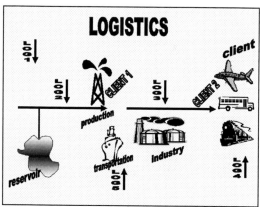

Figure 6 –Logistics actions in the Oil Industry

The productive chain in Figure 6 covers the following stages in the E&P (Exploration and Production) phase:
- discover of oil reserves;
- delimitation of the reserves;

- production development;
- production operation.

In the phase of supply and distribution of derivatives, the productive process concentrates on crude oil and gas refining for distribution to the market.

The logistics activities comprise:

- LOG1- purchase of materials and equipment, transportation of cargo and personnel, support and road engineering, equipment maintenance, contracting for services;
- LOG2- distribution to the market of oil and gas produced (various modes);
- LOG3- same as LOG1;
- LOG4- supply and acquisition of crude oil or gas, transportation to refineries;
- LOG5- distribution of derivatives to wholesale and retail markets.

Internally, the complete integration of this Logistics chain may be understood as the phase of Integrated Logistics, where the logistics resources from the various segmented logistics within an oil company (our example) are shared.

Depending on the size of the company, the differentiation among the different types of logistics occurs in a more intense manner. However, not only the size of the organization is a defining variable. The culture, the independence of internal departments/divisions, the market and similar industries maturity, the economy (if it is heated or not), are key factors in the formatting of organizations' Logistics.

Externally, the complete integration with suppliers from various external interfaces may occur (the situation in Figure 7).

One difference between Integrated Logistics and Supply Chain Management, according to Banfield (1999), rests on the external integration with suppliers and clients: Relationships / external alliances with partners are established and they involve sharing information and actions, differently from what happens in conventional systems. These relationships create a complex dependency between the internal and external parts of the chain. In other types of companies, such as service companies, where there may be companies dedicated to logistics exclusively, Integrated Logistics is handled differently as compared to its handling in transformation / production companies. The external interfaces may be proportionally greater and the dependency on external variables may be more influential.

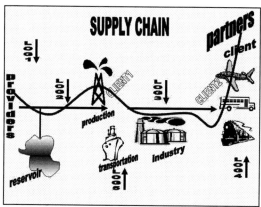

Figure 7 – Going from Integrated Logistics to the Supply Chain

Thus, in this chapter we have developed understanding of some concepts in Logistics as well as shown examples in the industry at large. In doing so, our objective was to place Logistics within the contextual variety of the business world.

2 – The cost of shortages

According to the dictionary (Holanda, 1997), shortage means "absence, lack, imperfection, defectiveness..." What does this mean then, in the logistics flow?

In the business sense, for each type of company and product, shortage has a specific meaning. In mass production companies, for example, shortage of a component may stop production, delay a product revenue, and bring about unsold end products. In technology companies, there may be other effects, such as idleness of their researchers. However, in this case, researchers could alternatively dedicate their time to other tasks that do not directly depend on the shortage, be it a physical, component-related or input shortage.

According to Schechter (1998), a successful process results in having the parts in the correct type and quantity at the right times. An overvaluation of quantities causes an excess of stock and obsolescence, while too conservative projections may result in shortages ("stock-outs") and losses to the consumers. Going further, Schulz (1999), based on studies by Ziebach Logistics Consultants, states that an increase of 1% in the error rate increases the logistics cost by 10%. Among the errors considered in the study are costs of lack of product delivery to clients, which breaks the Supply Chain.

In logistics companies, or even in the Logistics of the companies, a shortage may be related to the generation of end products themselves (Supply Logistics) or the distribution of products to end clients, the consumers. If Logistics is understood as the movement of goods and their availability for end users, shortage means that the main product of the logistics company was not produced or was not delivered, which reduces the revenue of the whole.

And how can we evaluate the cost of shortages? What is the true value of lack of a production component, or part of a productive system?

One way to answer this question is by making an analogy with Bachelard's (1984) words in the context of the Philosophy of

Science. According to him, the real is nothing more than its realization. It seems that something real is only instructive and safe if it has been materialized; above all, if it has been placed in its correct context, in its order of progressive creation. Although the philosopher is not directly referring to Logistics, his idea easily applies to our context.

That is, in the analysis of cost of shortages, the core issue is its materialization—the NON-operation of the productive chain because of there are shortages.

Thus, in Inbound Logistics, a shortage causes non-operation (no production of a product, for example), affecting the margin, as Figure 8 illustrates.

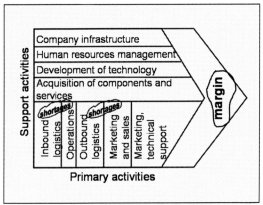

Adapted from Porter (1990)
Figure 8 – Areas of shortages

In Outbound Logistics, a shortage causes no-sale (an empty shelf, for example), also causing reduction of the margin.

The art or technique of managing this logistics "trade-off" is by establishing, beforehand, service levels for the possible shortages or quantities of physical materials, or even of resources or services (maintenance, inspection, etc.), both in Inbound and Outbound Logistics. This should happen in such a way that the final cost be minimum. Better predictability processes allow logistics people to estimate quantities that may absorb any eventual shortage in any of the links in the supply chain. This becomes more difficult and risky in processes with higher degrees of risk and unpredictability.

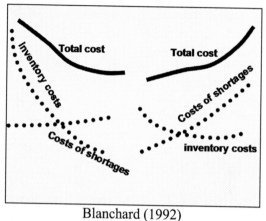

Blanchard (1992)
Figure 9 – Variations of stock risks and costs

Yet, shortage cost graphs are not always stable. They vary for each moment and degree of risk in the system. They get sharper to one side or the other, as Figure 9 shows.

The different slopes of the graphs, function of the variable 'quantity' (items, resources) on the horizontal axis, shows how critical the analysis of stock safety level is.   It requires sensibility to reach adequacy. As such, the issue should not be approached by means of minimizing equations, unless they are taken in their probabilistic scope.   I say so because risks are random variables and distort deterministic models.

While discussing the purpose of stocks, Disney (1997) asked us to consider that the primary purpose of stock is to serve as a fender for time delays. Stocks offer a better level of consumer service, by making goods available on the shop shelves, or anesthetics in the operating rooms of hospitals. He went on to say that it is undesirable to have a "stock out" situation (lack of stock) because the consumer will be lost to another business and part of the market will be lost. Therefore, according to him, stocks should be sufficient to cover variations and delay times.

Other aspects involved in shortage control are the linearity of the shortage and product, and alternatives to shortages.

Shortages are not always linearly dependent on production, because there may be a productive alternative of another product, the anticipation of another assembly line, or any other productive alternative that does not cause a direct, accentuated loss.

Also, the concept of shortage does not limit itself to the product or physical media, but happens whenever a resource, of any nature, necessary for the composition of a product or service, is not available in the quantity, specification, time or correct place. These attributions are permanently coupled to Logistics.

On the other hand, given the example of the productive chain in the Exploration and Production of Hydrocarbons in the Oil Industry, two points should be considered:

- A shortage stops the operation of the equipment, which results in payments without activity (this would be the case of lack of bits for the drilling rigs, for example) in the order of thousands of monetary units per day.
- A shortage delays the beginning of production in an oil field, causing revenue deferrals.

These two situations are presented in Figure 10.

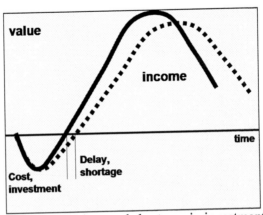

Figure 10 – Delays and shortages in investment:
Their impact on revenue

The lower and most displaced to the right graph represents the delay in time or shortage with the consequent reduction in revenue. Thus the values of inputs and materials in the Inbound Logistics have distinct impacts on the productive chain and production revenues. Such dimensions should be taken into account in establishing the stock levels in a logistic system. They impact as much or perhaps more than the value of the stock itself, creating the concept of impact of stocks and shortages on the productive cycle.

Shortages, which represent cost, should be calculated by projecting the two financial flows in dotted lines, that is, the flow without the occurrence of shortages (therefore, with enough stock as to avoid shortage); and the flow with the existence of shortage, represented by the full line.

The difference in value of these two flows, converted to the present value, is considered the cost of shortage.

Another type of cost derives from the comparison between the cost of shortage and the stock of services or materials, keeping the time basis constant. This treatment, illustred by Figure 11, is not linear neither deterministic, but probabilistic, since the facts and the anomalies are not continuously repeated, but show unpredictable variations.

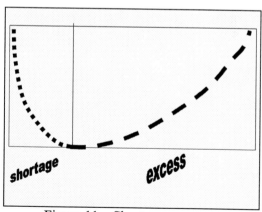

Figure 11 – Shortage or excess

In most cases and in general, the value of shortages is greater than the value of stocks for a given unit of measurement and initial time interval. The behavior of these two values, across time, may lead to distinct strategies and differentiated approaches to contingencies and necessary redundancies.

The slope of the curve that represents the cost of shortages is steeper than that relative to the cost of stocks. Thus, in general, protection against shortages is more relevant than against excessive stock. Neither is good, but both are real.

Therefore, the synergetic tie between the productive chain and the logistic flow creates a competitive differential in a world where small profit margins may mean survival. In other words, the productive and logistics chains may be considered partners with the same goals (even though less than in the case of internal clients). They break paradigms toward optimum partial and individual results and are always geared toward the best overall result.

3 – Management of Nodes in the Logistics Network

With the growth of a company's activities and its consequent horizontal multiplication (repeated processes occur in several separate geographic points), appeared the natural intention of optimizing common issues. Logistics resources, as for example, the supply of materials, are among these issues.

Markets are dynamic and there is no guarantee that there will always be suppliers and purchasers in sufficient numbers to assure a perfectly elastic market. Therefore, in case there is not a clear and defined criterion, when there are various consumption points in the same company and various external suppliers of a determined input or resource or product, there is risk of internal competition among consumers or users. Consequently, the supply of critical items for the points that add greater value to the set of the company's business is not guaranteed. In other words, if two points need the same product at close times, there is a chance of one being chosen over the other. Worse. It might be exactly the point that does not have the highest internal priority, delaying the other's supply and creating a relative reduction of the overall value of production, as well as a lower return on the investment made.

Figure 12 shows a conventional supplier scheme.

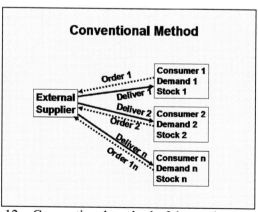

Figure 12 – Conventional method of demand management

According to it, each consumption point analyzes its demand and issues orders to supply it, constituting its own stock (including individual safety stock). This process seeks to ensure the operation of a point of consumption.

From the opportunities for optimization created by the conventional system in Figure 12, arose the concept of MANAGEMENT OF NODES IN THE LOGISTICS NETWORK or more simply MANAGEMENT OF NODES.

Figure 13 schematizes a network node, where the MANAGER of the NODE, which does not have any physical stock, receives information about demand from the various consumption points, analyzing and issuing only one order for each already consolidated external supplier.

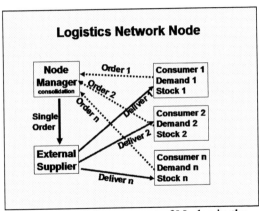

Figure 13 – Management of Nodes in the Logistics network

It takes into account that the sum of the physical stock of each consumption point does not need to have the same level as if all consumption points were operating independently, because they can benefit, laterally, from the stock of the "neighbor consumption point", in case of contingencies.

The Manager of the Node does not have physical stocks, but works only with information, optimizing the process of adequately supplying the points at a minimum cost. The group of Node Managers is a very small group of people, who share the profile of project managers and have good knowledge of the business as well as of stock management.

Therefore, the difference between the two schemes (12 and 13) rests on the sharing of the quantitative stock (as shown in Figure 13), even though the physical stock was originally available in each geographical consumption point. Actually, only information is common, and there is no creation of additional stock.

Figure 14 illustrates a theoretical scheme for resource sharing that supports the concept of "Network Node." Although it does not endure an advanced mathematical basis (future studies could address the issue), it allows us to further analyze the idea. It shows four vehicles riding down a road.

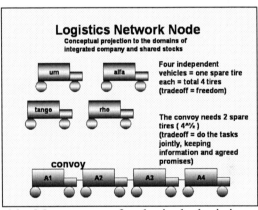

Figure 14 – Management of nodes in the logistics network

If they ride independently, each vehicle would need one spare tire to ensure a guaranteed service level, taking into account the risk of a puncture in one of the four tires of each vehicle.

Keeping the same level of risk, if the four vehicles ride on the same road, on the same trajectory, but in a convoy system, that is together, without getting separated, two tires would bring the same service level as previously stipulated. This would be possible because they could share resources if necessary.The idea can also be representend in a mathematical form, had it related autonomous to shared resources in a square root:

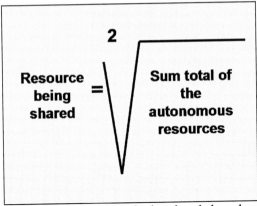

Figure 15 – Relation between isolated and shared resources

From the line of reasoning we have developed, we may infer that there is a logistics trade-off that requires explanation:

Advantages of driving in convoy	Disadvantages of driving in convoy
Shared risks	Less autonomy
Lower quantity of total resources	Lower final speed
Mutual support	Commitment for the lower index

In other words, what we have called management of nodes in the network means generating demands of a given resource, with special characteristics; consolidating them; and issuing materials delivery orders, with characteristics like

- Group material value greater than X monetary units, the cut-off point being that which divides the set of materials into 20% of the items and 80% of the value of the materials moved in a given period of time;
- More than one user or consumer;
- Complexity of the supplier market;
- Criticality or impact on the continuity and operational service level.

These conditions, applied to the supply of materials and equipment to any productive process, comprises an important factor for industrial gain: Standardization.

Standardization of specifications and reduction of varieties (at a limit that is rational and does not produce operational constraints) are special tools for cost reduction in the logistics cycle. They generate savings in various categories.

These tools bring to light a relevant issue. In case of external supply crises, they create a joint mass that allows prioritizations and redirection of materials among internal users. This would be possible even if there is need to negotiate and if postponements occur, because there is sufficient quantity and points to absorb business variations (delays in combined resources => transportation, personnel, maintenance etc.). Such movement procedure is called internal transference of materials among operation units and its total does not indicate that there is more or less correlated efficiency. It is simply a tool to meet instances of instability without increasing stocks. It gives flexibility, an effect similar to what happens in Microeconomics, when one talks of elastic markets and the capacity to absorb oscillations in demand and offer.

To select materials which may take part in the node management system, I suggest that, once a matrix for the parameters of interest has been put together, each group of materials should undergo continuous analyses as illustrated in Figure 16. This procedure would allow us to classify the materials that should be submitted to node management.

Figure 16 shows a decision matrix. It needs to contain parameters that ensure control items for the main productive process, that is, the company's business.

In other words, the supply of materials and equipment should be perfectly tied to the business productive cycle, adjusting and optimizing the indicators of the principal system themselves, as far as they are not undermined. This means that the priority is not that of supply, but of the business, because whatever intended or promised optimization in supply only will have little importance compared to the main productive process, that is, to operate and distribute production for external clients (those who pay).

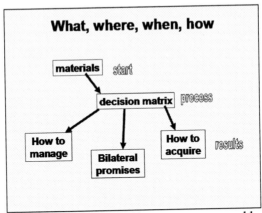

Figure 16 – Decision matrix of how to manage and buy stocks

Proper functioning of the system depends on the capacity of each consumer point to exercise the role of manager of groups for distinct materials. Only then there can be reciprocal commitment between the parts involved. Each one of them shares the roles of user and manager, whenever possible. Put in another way, 'to use' and 'to manufacture' concomitantly help those involved to exercise commitment, increasing the process efficiency (which is based on resources sharing and distributed gains).

Management of nodes confirms in practice the value of sharing resources. It shows that when resource sharing is practiced according to previously agreed mechanisms and criteria, it may provide a systematic rationalization for Supply Logistics, without removing business capacity from each use point. It only requires adequate planning, and understanding among participants, because everyone pursues the same objective: A minimum final cost and guaranteed levels of service. Besides, management of nodes also allows the strength of a user company to be used in the market not only in purchase negotiations but also in the logistics optimization of movement and transportation, by means of the scale variable.

One of the significant factors of this model is the induced standardization of materials or reduction of varieties, because the capacity of analyzing different demands, their peculiarities and similarities, is given to consolidators. This allows them to evaluate the variety of specifications and to propose a reduction of varieties in the technical specifications. Additionally, they can even choose a range of materials to replace the variety, whenever the value of the stock is significant and economical. If this is the case, the consolidators can then accept alternative specifications to reduce the varieties.

Another benefit of this model is the optimization of cargo and transportation, because once the demands are in hands, cargos may be optimized so as to reduce costs for both sides, that is, for suppliers and users.

Bellow follows the main system indicators:

- Stock coverage for material items, in number of months;
- Percentage of hits between estimated demand and the actual consumption, per requesting use point;
- Index of response time between the node and the manager, in agreed % by the actual achieved time;
- Total stock value;
- Cost of the managing node.

The model also allows us to deal with other functions or resources as far as adaptations are implemented and resources are not put before the productive process itself, but become parts of it, in a total Supply Chain view.

Some of the aspects that need to be addressed include:

- Difficulty in obtaining information at the right time;
- Avoidable internal transfers;
- Difficulty in obtaining a reduction of variety or standardization;
- Resistance in accepting to behave as a node or the desire to be just a user;

- False perception of non-autonomy from the core business;
- Systems difficulties for cost distribution, mainly on the part of those who act as nodes.

Ultimately, management of nodes is a management tool that brings important business gains and offers management features against losses. It can provide a significant economy in intensely competitive environments.

It is worth stressing that what applies to internal units within a company may be extrapolated to companies of the same group or, even to different companies of separate groups, provided that they have suitable agreements and management.

4 – Logistics Indicators

To establish indicators for a group of activities or function, it is necessary, first, to explain the definition and amplitude of these activities or functions. If Logistics is the part of the supply chain that implements and controls the efficient and effective flow and stocking of goods, services and related information, from the point of origin to the point of consumption, seeking to meet the consumers' requirements, its indicators relate to the following variables:

- Quality, integrity, and checking of quantity and specifications;
- Costs of the logistics process;
- Term of each sub-activity and how attractive it is for the client;
- Service or suitable level of response;
- Flexibility, relative to the adaptations, to the requesting group, and to environmental restrictions;
- Safety, with respect to the standards and certainties of no accidents and no losses;
- Ethics of those who perform in the activity;
- Index of client satisfaction.

Such indicators may be related to the results and processes of:

- Transportation;
- Acquisition of materials and parts;
- Stock Management;
- Warehousing Management;
- Maintenance management;
- Infrastructure Engineering;
- Physical Distribution.

They may also be related to all other areas of logistics action in a given environment, as far as the peculiarities of each application are respected.

Each of these indicators branches off in three levels: The managerial, tactical, and operational levels. The management indicators, which are strategic, may include the overall results, client satisfaction etc. The operational indicators, which are detailed and obtained in each stage of each process, seek to measure activities and allow the optimization, sharing and reorganization of actions.

In the case of the logistics indicators, frequent trade-offs are common. An increase in the speed of delivery may increase costs, but it also increases client satisfaction, opening new markets. Similarly, a reduction in the speed of delivery may reduce costs and, consequently, the final price to the client too, increasing its attractiveness. Therefore, there is demand for each type of results, which gives rise to a third feature— "flexibility"-- or even to a fourth —"mix solutions"—for each type of client. It is thus necessary to have a management and a strategy for each market and demand situations, placing the company in the range and niches suitable to generate survival, competition, and adaptability.

For example, let's ask ourselves the following questions: When could delivery time or the certainty of delivery within the agreed time be more important than the physical integrity and quality of the product? What is the relative importance value among the alternative delivery times? How much are we prepared to pay for each one of these variables?

Now, let's take the following simulated scenario:

Client 1 acquires perishable products in bulk, with a low unit value;

Client 2 acquires durable, sensitive, electronic goods and keeps a stock as an operational guarantee;

Client 3 acquires materials and equipment for an asset construction project, such as an offshore oil rig or an industrial production manufacturing plant;

For each one of the cited types of demand there is a distinct approach and the indicators receive a differentiated relative importance.

For Client 1, delivery time certainty is essential, because perishability eliminates the value of the product, if delivery happens at longer times than the agreed.

For Client 2, delivery time certainty does not have such relevance, but the intrinsic quality and reliability of the components are essential, because this is a case of replacement of stock levels for continuous consumption.

For Client 3, the project management indicators grow in importance, without neglecting the compatibility among those involved. This is so because it is a case that requires synchronization of various chronograms of materials, services and equipment from separate suppliers.

And so on and so forth. Each client or demand justifies a greater effort for a determined group of variables, indicators, and goals, with controls that need to be established and systematically pursued.

Furthermore, a system of logistics indicators should consider business factors that are commented or passed on by suppliers and clients such as

- costs (payments, receivables, profits, volume, and return on investments);
- cycle time (order cycle, replacement cycle);
- technology (quantity in application, innovation index);
- market participation;
- intrinsic quality of the products delivered;
- response time;
- cost per activity;
- stock turnover;
- quantity of deliveries on planned dates;
- client satisfaction;
- facility to place orders;
- facility to follow or track orders;

- administrative flexibility for clients;
- post-sales technical support.

These examples and others that I encountered in my professional experience indicate that it is possible to adopt a system of measurement for each client, or group of activities or functions, or category of logistics resources. Such a system allows us to follow up several issues related to numbers and goals.

For each time period, established by upper management, two types of meetings are recommended:

1- A meeting to follow up and critique current indicators;
2- A meeting to review (include or remove) indicators in the system.

Thus, if you are going to work with indicators, you should follow steps one to five, as listed below:

1. Identify
2. Select
3. Measure
4. Correct
5. Adjust

Indicators should be monitored and used as management tools. Otherwise, they do not comply with their basic role, which is to point out the state, situation, tendency, and comparison.

An excess of indicators is not recommended, but the use of a few and good measures, which truly express what we wish to control and apply corrective actions to, if it is the case, are.

These indicators should have two characteristics:

A view of responsibility;
A view of control or accountability.

For example, let's consider an indicator that contains the performance of a supplier of materials and equipment, with its composition:

Supply performance (I) = compliance + punctuality + service + innovation + price

Each one of the components has a concept, a value range, and allows follow up across time, for each supplier.

- Compliance = that which was requested was delivered, in the right specifications and quantities;
- Punctuality = the agreed delivery time was complied with;
- Service = time and quality of the responses in business and technical interactions;
- Innovation = expansion in the business processes and development of technologies / products;
- Price = maintenance or reduction of prices across time.

The system may have various characteristics, such as the evaluation of the component variables after the acquired product is delivered and used. Also, the evaluations may consider problems or qualities in such a manner that the suppliers may be rewarded with indexes above expectations. Finally, variables can be weighted according to their relevance, which empowers those supplier who have a greater impact on the productive chain they will supply for.

Another approach is to numerically evaluate the variables according to costs, including cost of shortages. The formula would be:

Total cost (activity) = cost of safety stock + cost of no service

This concept applies well to internal suppliers, who need to keep stocks for certain production phases. They need to establish sufficient safety stock levels to avoid shortages or no services, since cost of shortages and of no services are substantially greater than the cost of stocks.

5 – Logistics Benchmarking

Benchmarking can be defined as a process that systematically searches for information and for measures of the performance-related best practices in the market. It seeks continuous improvement by planning changes geared toward gaining market leadership or by running comparisons with similar practices.

Therefore, doing benchmarking means more than simply measuring performance, but running a continuous process that reveals the state of a corporation or function. To run this process, we draw on the logistics indicators and their relative position, as well as that of the practices. This allows a careful analysis of the causes of such a state and levers a process of adaptation or change. The fundamental issue is to get to know how market leaders act and what the best market practices for a determined class of indicators are. Figure 17 represents this process.

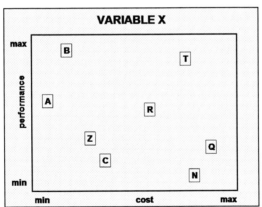

Figure 17 – Distribution of performance x cost in a benchmarking diagram

Initially, when a similar process has never been executed, it is recommended that we learn about its position in the market, as compared to other competitors and to the market leaders.

Such a process will allow us to see what is the corporation's or business unit's relative position for each variable or indicator, for example, performance x cost, in a static measurement.

Let's take the scenario in Figure 18 and imagine that company C is the one under analysis. The figure shows that there is a large room for improvement in C's processes, strategies or actions. However, this realization is not enough.

A second step would involve seeking to know C's comparative progress across time, as a function of the efficacy of the actions planned and executed. This could be done by contrasting its comparative evolution with the actions taken for recovery of the position.

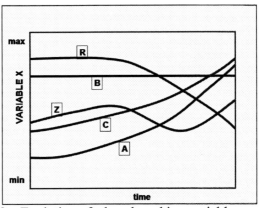

Figure 18 – Evolution of a benchmarking variable according to a comparison among different companies across time

Across time, company C, the object of the previous analysis, organized changes and improved its relative position in the market for variable X (which may be the performance + cost pair, for example). It incorporated and adopted practices learned from the benchmarking process and already in use by the market leaders, for variable X.

With the arrival of Total Quality Management, various concepts were directed to continuous improvement processes and PDCA cycles (Plan, Do, Control, Act). Consequently, all efforts were on the logistics concepts that direct these variables, which are considered essential and are understood by various sections of society (consumers, companies, service providers, government, shareholders etc.). The client's viewpoint comes to rule in an unconditional manner, which reverses the practice of implementing actions without considering the client's needs. A reversal of this magnitude runs the risk of exaggeration, but entails, without any doubt, a significant cultural change.

To prepare a benchmark, it is fundamental to consider some questions. Namely:

- Who are the true competitors? Who are the market leaders?
- How do they think?
- How to prepare long term plans, taking into account the variables that one is willing to consider?
- What are the best practices? Which indicators will be key to the comparisons?
- What are the processes resulting from the analyses and comparisons?
- In what parts are changes necessary?
- Which changes are fundamental and which are easy or difficult? How much effort each change will require?
- What is the expected return for each change, individually? Is it possible to make an economic analysis, at least estimated, involving the costs and returns, as if it were a Net Present Value?
- Is there internal resistance from people toward the implementation of the changes? What about culture? Working environment?
- What is the time of return for each change?

In other words, a benchmarking process should incorporate key or critical indicators connected to the corporation's results, or, its survival. It requires detachment from defensive attitudes or "watching one's back" behaviors, as well as the capacity to hear unsettling truths. Only then effective corrective actions can be taken.

There are different types of benchmarkings:

- Competitive benchmarking, which compares the performance of companies in similar activities, even if they deal with distinct products;
- Process benchmarking, which identifies the best practices related to functions, independently of the area in which these functions are;
- Combined competitive and process benchmarking, which involves both types of actions previously described.

Every benchmarking should aim at identifying areas for improvement and should result in a work program geared at fulfilling the gaps identified and accepted as fundamental for the survival of the corporation.

To exemplify these ideas, I introduce an example of Research for Benchmarking in Supply Chain Management. Because the example only draws on a sample and does not cover a typical complete data set, its purpose is simply to illustrate the kind of questions involved in the process.

Name of the Organization:_____
Address:_____
Telephone:_____
Fax:_____
Name of its Representative:_____
E-mail:_____

1. What is the range or business area which best characterizes your enterprise?

Military ( )
Automotive ( )
Computers, Hardware ( )
Computers, Software ( )
Education ( )
Bank, Finances ( )
Mining ( )

Government ( )
Health ( )
Insurance ( )
Manufacture ( )
Games and entertainment ( )
Petroleum and Petrochemicals( )
Pharmaceuticals ( )
Distribution ( )
Telecommunications ( )
None of the above ( )

2. What is your hierarchical position in the organization?

Buyer ( )
Purchases Supervisor ( )
Demand Planning ( )
Engineering ( )
Manager ( )
Director ( )

3. What is the gross revenue of your company, per year, in US$ billions?

0 to 0.2 ( )
0.2 to 0.5 ( )
0.5 to 1 ( )
1 to 5 ( )
5 to 10 ( )
10 to 20 ( )
20 to 50 ( )
More than 50 ( )

4. Does your organization execute projects internally?

yes ( )

no ( )

5. Does your organization use third parties for any part of the manufacturing process?

yes ( )   what % in value?_____
no ( )

6. Does your organization control qualification of the components and vendor list of outsourced projects?

yes ( )   all ( )   high value ( )   standardization ( )   special projects ( )
no ( )

7. Does your organization inspect and test the sub-products or resources manufactured by third parties?

yes ( )   all ( )   high value ( )   standardization ( )   special projects ( )
no ( )

8. What are the processes used in your organization to ensure the quality of products or resources manufactured by third parties?

alliances ( )
at the end of the project or upon delivery ( )
sample auditing ( )
periodic inspection ( )
inspection and release per stage developed ( )
variable cost ( )

9. What mechanisms does your organization use to ensure the flow of parts and resources that are bottlenecks in the supply chain of suppliers and sub-suppliers?

-contracts with bonuses and penalties? ( )
-direct negotiations with sub-suppliers ? ( )
-negotiation committee involving suppliers and
 sub-suppliers ? ( )
-contracting of third parties to control and inspect
  sub-suppliers ? ( )

10. What is the relative work force (or percentage) considering the supply chain groups and the total force of the company (numer of employees or total sum of their compensations)?

0 to 1 ( )
1 to 5 ( )
5 to 10 ( )
10 to 20 ( )
20 to 50 ( )
More than 50 ( )

11. What are the contingency mechanisms used by your organization in case of failures in the supply chain by third parties?

_____

12. Are there redundancy mechanisms for critical logistics systems? Which?

_____

Armando Cavanha

6 – Internal client or partner

While the world already practices external partnerships with companies outside the limits of their own domains and adopt a supply chain perspective (Figure 19), there are still people who think and debate as if they were internal clients or as if one and the other were the end objectives (Figure 20).

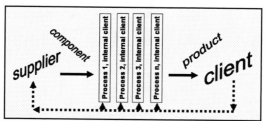

Figure 19 – Schematic representation of a productive flow

Why? Would there be misleading interpretations of basic concepts in Total Quality, such as clients, products, and processes? What are the true objectives and clients of a given organization? Who pays for the product or services that an organization produces? The internal client? (Figure 20) Or the external client? Internally, the processes to obtain parts of a product depend on various players who are not clients, but partners.

Figure 20 – Schematic representation of internal clients and a team in partnership

If internal players do not produce in a manner that is sufficient or aligned with the organization's purpose, they can be replaced. The same does not happen with external clients, who efficient or not, cannot be changed. External clients (or simply put, clients), should always be attended to. Otherwise they change their suppliers.

Furthermore, the internal relationship among processes should not follow the same style adopted for external clients (those who pay). It is somewhat exaggerated to work with internal agents as if they were external, except for training purposes or the establishment of internal goals. Without clarity about the roles played, there may be distortions, internal competition and squabbling.   This ends up producing total costs greater than those that are necessary as well as conflicts among segments of the same organization.

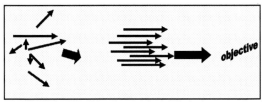

Figure 21 – Schematic representation of the vectors' alignment

Because those responsible for sub-processes are not clients and suppliers, but partners, internal vectors, or the objectives of those responsible for sub-processes, should be aligned with the same purpose. The resultant is a greater force in the direction and sense of the vectors because of such an alignment (Figure 21). It follows the path of the true client, who is external, who generates cash, market, employment, salaries, and profits, and justifies everyone's presence within an organization. To exemplify this idea, imagine a lawyer who works in a famous hamburger company. When someone asks him/her about what s/he does in the company, his/her answer goes "I sell fast food." Such an answer shows how much the lawyer is aligned with the company's mission.   It is this alignment which characterizes successful companies.

A similar situation would be to ask the owner of a bakery who is his/her clients and suppliers at the moment s/he hires a baker. Wouldn't s/he say that the one who puts the bread in the oven is the client of the one who prepares the dough?

In an organization, without a good understanding of how much and how each one contributes with the necessary alignment and internal clarification of tasks, goals and common objectives, one runs the risk of creating a paradox such as the "BURIDAN'S ASS" (Jean Buridan, 14th century philosopher), which states that if an ass were placed *"exactly in the middle of two stacks of hay of equal size and quality, it would starve to death because it would be uncapable of making any rational decision to start eating one or the other."* Aristotle was the first to mention this paradox. He referred to a man who would die of hunger and thirst because he would remain unmoved when positioned exactly between food and drink. Figure 22 illustrates the idea.

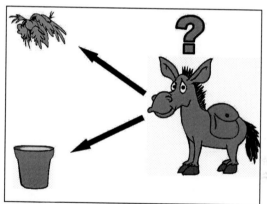

Figure 22 – Schematic representation of the Buridan's ass

7 – Stocks of services x stocks of materials

Companies generally stock up materials, resources or inputs to ensure a productive operating capacity. To stock up means to be prepared for fluctuations in supply, due to whatever reason, aiming at protecting the most expensive link in the productive chain: Production itself most times. On the other hand, if companies stock up finished products, stocking up means guaranteeing the availability of products for sale on the shelves, generating revenue, and retaining clients.

In the case of enterprises or constructions where there are materials / equipment and services, in some instances they acquire materials with built-in services and in others services with built-in materials, both contracted from the same supplier. In these cases, the responsibility is generally given to one contractor only to reduce wastes of time and outsource service management completely.

However, instead of minimizing risks and disagreements, this method of contracting may sometimes cause greater costs compared to contracting two separate parties. That is, contracting services from one supplier and purchasing materials from another. This method may be recommended when there is no market specialization for the desired combination, or when packers make excessive profits.

In this case, contracting services from one company and acquiring materials from another is acceptable. The management of the parties can be done by one's own personnel or even by contracted employees. Some cases require an evaluation of the actual costs of a process, not only of the apparent ones, because if there are delays of services for materials available, there will be stocks of materials; on the other hand, if there are delays of materials for services available, there will be stocks of services.

In Figure 23, the upper arrows show materials delivery, while the lower arrows of each time line represent the delivery of services. Only in the third situation (the last arrow), services and materials are received simultaneously.

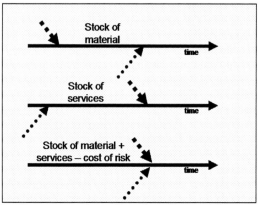

Figure 23 – Representation of stocks of materials, services, and risks in package contracts

Some service companies that have already experienced unforeseen additional costs include stand-by costs in the contracts. That is, the cost of immobilizing their resources, whether in production or waiting time. The responsibility falls on whom is receiving the contracted services and may not be using them suitably.

The risk of this type of cost is common in large undertakings. To decide for one or other modality of stock, companies should use the expected values of these occurrences (probability x cost) as good alternatives to compare existing modalities.

Cost = materials + services + [(100 - risk %) x time x stand-by]

The third parcel represents the contingency cost, which includes the probability of any divergence occurring in the flows of materials and services that were contracted separately, multiplied by the time this situation will possibly last and by the stand-by cost per unit.

On stratified costs, as compared to packaged costs by a third party, lies the true difference between the two situations: To purchase materials and services separately and cope with contingency costs or to contract a complete package that in-builts the global cost and risk offered by just one supplier.

To protect their capacity of choosing one or the other modality of stock, according to each's advantages and disadvantages, some companies prefer to operate with both systems, purposely balancing one and the other.

Also, such strategy allows flow and change from one modality to the other with great ease, because it keeps functional and packaged contracts in operation. If necessary, an increase in tasks and cargos in the contracts will suffice.

Ultimately, stocks of services and stocks of materials are only stocks. They are necessary evils that should not be managed by their quantitative dimensions. That is, by their capacity of accumulating items to protect a system. They should, above all, be managed according to their essences of use, their existing characteristics and alternative possibilities of contracting. This is what transforms stocks into strategic game pieces for the protection of productive systems.

8 – Complexity x Criticality

The set of acquisitions of goods and services is heterogeneous and entails characteristic sub-sets that are controlled by different variables: Quality, deadlines, support, size of the supplier, quantity of suppliers, technologies involved, etc.

There are innumerable ways of organizing these sub-sets; however, one methodology, in especial, calls attention because of the applicability of its resolution--the binomial complexity versus criticality.

The first term, complexity, relates to how complex the supplier market is for the acquisition of a given sub-set. It comprises the following vectors:

- Number of suppliers available;
- Technologies involved in the productive process;
- Production risks or availability of resources;
- Risks of uncontrolled price fluctuations;
- The possibility of making arrangements among suppliers and cartels or of establishing ties among suppliers and business competitors.

If we examine these variables, we can classify each sub-set of acquisitions according to their relative degree of complexity, on a scale from 0 to 100% (each sub-set will have a greater or lesser intensity of complexity relative to each other).

The second term, criticality, refers to the use or application of the material or service item and to the domain to which it belongs. That is, we should examine if the item is part of the main internal process as an accessory or as a fundamental element, on a scale of different intermediate levels of criticality. Criticality comprises then the following vectors:

- How the item participates in essential productive processes;
- Intrinsic technology of the item;
- Replaceability of the item;

- Serial or parallel production (no wait time for components).

If the two sub-sets or categories of purchases and services are placed along two axes, on relative scales from 0 to 100%, being the horizontal axis for criticality and the vertical one for complexity, a graph of relationships may be plotted as in Figure 24:

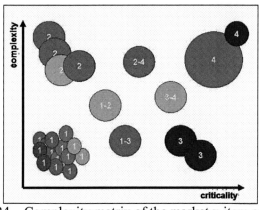

Figure 24 – Complexity matrix of the market x item criticality

Acquisition items entered the graph according to their relative complexity and criticality. The diameter of each sphere represents the expected annual value of acquisitions. The darker the color, the greater the number of internal users of the same service items or materials is (different units, regions etc.). More complex and critical items tend to have a greater relative annual value, as well as be used by fewer internal units. However, this is not a rule, only a tendency.

A recommended way to approach the market, given the same axes and scales in the previous graph (Figure 24), would be the one represented in Figure 25. Such representation belongs to the public domain and is systematically used by specialized consultancies:

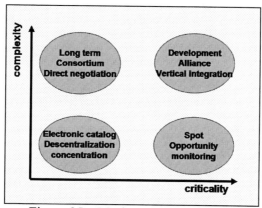

Figure 25 – Market approach matrix

Each quadrant has a distinct recommendation for approaching the supplier market. A very critical item and a very complex market leads to an alliance or partnership relationship, reaching the limits of acquisition from a supplier (integration), such is the supposed importance of the item. On the other hand, low criticality of application and low complexity of the market settles for a generic market. That is, a market which is not specific, is typical of electronic acquisitions, decentralizes orders, and focuses on the potential to reduce purchasing costs by sharing markets.

If the two graphs (Figures 24 and 25) are superimposed, an important tool for approaching a market becomes available. The resultant graph (Figure 26) shows what the best strategy for contracting each sub-set of purchases or services is. It is a dynamic graph and as such it should be updated and redone periodically, because

- the perceptions of complexity and criticality vary;
- suppliers appear and change often;
- quality and time of products and services vary;
- developments and new technologies alter the matrix;
- criticality depends on the phase of the productive chain and on the business momentum.

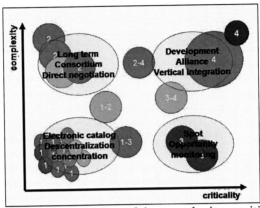

Figure 26 – Superposition of the complexity x criticality
matrices and of market approaches

Thus, to acquire materials or services for a productive chain, diversified manners of relationships should be observed, depending on how they refer to the material or service item and on how they relate to the supplier, as functions of the variables presented. There are restrictions to this approach, however, mainly:

- National, regional or local taxes;
- Generic legislation;
- Legislation specific to the type of company;
- Internal organization of acquisitions based on value levels per event.

Such restrictions may restrict the approach by categories, but should not take the focus away from organizing, qualifying and dealing with the more complex and critical subjects in differentiated manners.

To organize structure and management by categories of complexity and criticality constitutes a challenge in large corporations. Essential productive activities tend to resist this vision. They prefer to align all the critical resources with the results axis and persist in affirming that only by having control of the resources may they be held responsible for the results that are assigned to them.

This is not a situation unique to one or another corporation. Existing information indicate that this type of fragmented positioning occurs with very high frequency in large-volume and long-chain production environments.

One possible alternative would be to move noble and non-noble activities (those that are executed by other areas and become support activities) to the end activity, trying to integrate them completely. Consequently, this system would drive to an organization by business units or even by independent subsidiaries. In case this is not the true intention of the corporation, care should be taken to avoid excessive infra-structure costs and the disintegration of the areas, which would lead to an inevitable loss of synergy among them.

In other words, it is the paradigms of an organization and the oscillatory movements in its structure and management that keeps it alive. A simple method to avoid contrary tendencies is to rotate positions compulsorily, without time extensions, reducing territorial disputes.

Logistics strategies are management strategies, seen from the point-of-view of variables. These variables may relate to an organization's logistics values and dimensions or to a network of them.

Within the Supply Chain vision, a component / resource should flow from the most upstream phase of the productive/logistics process to the most downstream phase, that is, from the acquisition of parts and resources to the finished product's final client.

This flow should be as continuous as possible and should incorporate attributes such as quality, time, information and support, in sufficient amounts, so as to maintain the lowest possible loss of load throughout the flow's physical, informational or financial trajectory, without waste, and by adding value along the process, with a minimum risk of shortage, excess or unsuitability.

Once groups that require supply alliances have been chosen, the perfect relationship between suppliers and receivers, be them internal or external, resources and components, one after another, in the productive / logistics chain should be established. Such a relationship constitutes one of the substantial elements of laminar flow. Operators placed downstream from a process receive a semi-product and add their competence to it, until the resources and components transform it (together with the productive processes) into a saleable end product.

In the provisioning or acquisition of resources and components, transactional relationships are instantaneous; they relate to the moment or opportunity and are not good for sustaining laminar, continuous flows. When the acquisition of a resource or component is transformed into a part of the productive process itself, by the establishment of strategic alliances for example, the objective is a continuous and committed supply regime and its subsequent processes; or else, minimum variability of attributes, few interruptions and unsuitabilities.

Alliances are a win–win relationship, in which who supplies a product or service, jointly with the partners who receive it, discuss and make requirements feasible for both, without surprises. The continuous flow regime and the preventively altered regime are marks of success of alliances and long term commitments, and they are always present in profitable business relationships.

The selection and maintenance of allies are strategic tasks. In performing them, there is no room for experiments or weak attempts, which have no evident attractiveness.

How to select a partner then? How to choose a partner, given the various options, and, at the same time, maintain, change and adapt alliances?

The answer would be: By analyzing content. To do it, it is necessary to focus on suppliers' essential variables. Namely, their perspectives, market position, how they approach the main issues in the business relationship, mutual dependence, contingency, common and isolated technological developments, the possibility of developing patents and industrial innovations, among others, in stages prior to deciding which alliances to make.

In alliances, the interfaces among the processes are shared between suppliers and receivers, be them internal or external, in such a way that a mutual commitment and analyzed gains can be obtained by both parties. Figure 27 illustrates the processes. In it, additive interfaces refer to common activities and to those that are performed jointly, with time reduction, while in transactional activities, with waterproof interfaces, the total time extends itself along the total of each stage's complete times.

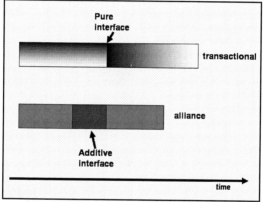

Figure 27 – Diagram of alliance and interface zones

Business alliances are important productivity tools, sensitive and compromising. All variables should be discussed, analyzed and registered, so as to allow gains in time and cycles of use, always keeping in mind that it is necessary to know how to go back to acting in a conventional and independent form, if the alliance does not progress. Entering into an alliance requires strategy, elasticity, and contingency.

To establish alliances, the following stages should be observed:

1- Analysis of attractiveness.

- Quantify mutual dependence between the parties;
- Align technical project alternatives;
- Project demands for the next years--quantity and value;

- Analyze business opportunitie and market;
- In the case of more than one supplier, analyze the modality of selection of partners;
- Analyze the inclusion or not of added services and packages; or separate hardware and software.

2- Legal conditions.

- Analyze restrictions and qualifications to make alliances;
- Examine similar contracts with other companies, or references;
- Examine the roles of the parties, limits, flexibility of use, technical and business options;
- Examine contingencies and rescission mechanisms;
- Consider mandatory or elective use by Business Units.

3- Proposal of business agreement administration by upper management.

4- Negotiation with possible allies, remembering the aspects listed below:

- Monitoring of the contract (prices, terms , support, level of development ...);
- Development of new technologies;
- Conditions for sales of products developed jointly with third parties;
- Joint patents? Rights, profits...
- Level of information sharing (internal costs ...);
- Changes in current practices
  - o A - purchase of hardware+spares+stocks and run operation with own employees;
  - o B -   contract a complete function, paying piecework for the work actually produced;
- Need to equate the best practices for each situation, equipment, resources + market, independently of alliances with A or B.

Another relevant subject within this context of strategies is the value chain and its sub-divisions, aiming at achieving end products. A related theme would be "procurement to pay" (P2P), which includes current integrated information systems now available for business markets. P2P seeks to integrate activities from start to finish. Some classical dilemmas by sub-systems of procurement teams could be taken as examples. One would be the simplified trade-off "just buy and just expedite"; or, "buy and expedite simultaneously," as illustrated by Figure 28:

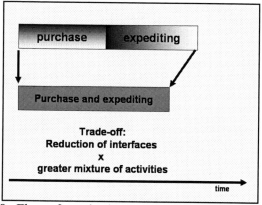

Figure 28 –Flow of purchasing by function and by procuring to pay

Without any doubt, there are advantages and disadvantages in each of the options. The option that subdivides tasks and individuals increases specialization in one sub-task and the sense of serial production of items, stimulating quantitative productivity. On the other hand, it does not stimulate the quality of each sub-product delivered, although it is possible, because another individual performs the next sub-stage.

The other option, in which the same individual produces from start to finish, increases quality of end product delivery, but does not encourage productivity, because the same person deals with different subjects, of lesser or greater importance, simultaneously, in the same productive chain. This generates losses.

Another current dilemma in procurement is how to classify purchases, if by clients or by seller (by categories), which also leads to a logistics trade-off.

In this case, while the classification by clients encourages the solution of individual problems, the classification by categories, encourages a deeper knowledge of the supplier market.

The first illustration in Figure 29 shows the first model or the classification of purchases by client. In it, there is an intense and direct connection between the client and related purchases, which improves the search for solutions to specific problems. On the other hand, approaches to the market are duplicated, every buyer buys everything and does not specialize or know any market in depth, and sellers may take advantage of diverging information.

The second illustration in Figure 29 shows the classification of purchases by categories. This model improves the interface with the market, increases specialization, and reduces differences in the prices obtained. However, it also weakens the direct buyer- client connection, reduces knowledge of specific clients' demands, etc.

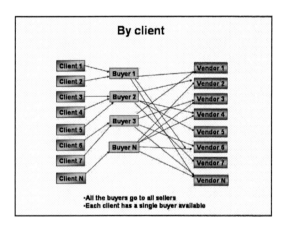

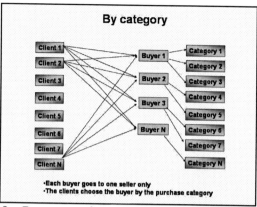

Figure 29 – Processes of acquisition: By client or by category

When the number of clients increases too much in relation to the number of buyers, or even sellers, the option naturally tends to the purchase by categories model; when the number of clients is lower, with greater values per purchase, the option tends to the purchases by client model.

Each case should be basically analyzed as a function of the following variables:

- Value per purchase;
- Total annual value;
- Number of clients;
- Number of buyers;
- Number of sellers;
- Client variation;
- Variation of sellers;
- Market Complexity;
- Specialty of the specifications;
- Impact of shortages on the productive processes;
- Use or not of buffer stocks;
- Level of negotiations required;
- Manufacturing times;
- Type of market, if elastic or specific;
- Buyers' specialization;

- Logistics time, distances, modals, intensity of management of expediting delivery.

A careful analysis of these and other variables allows the adoption of a model adjusted to each situation.

There are, however, possible management compensations for this model. For example, among other alternatives, a helpdesk could be exclusively designated to handle purchases by categories, and information system solutions could be adopted to allow clients to track processes step by step.

Another interesting strategy would be to plan a change of models from time to time, in an organized and discussed manner. All previous commitments made while operating in one previous model would be kept, until the processes that had begun in each situation were completed. This would oxygenate and renovate the adopted systematics, remove structural defects, among other benefits.

Obviously, the way in which the strategy is applied differentiates success from failure, because movements of such a nature need to count on the commitment and extra motivation by all involved.

9 –Information Systems and e-technology in Logistics

Electronic commerce has transformed operations and logistics management with greater speed than new concepts in Business Administration, Engineering and Logistics themselves. It has produced a variation in scope and business processes that has its own logics.

The time of physical processes does not match the speed of e-solutions. This fact brings large challenges, notably for Logistics. While our clients have fast and safe tools to order and track orders and payments, Logistics still transports goods by ground, sea or air and faces limited speed and operational restrictions for various physical, geographical, political and social reasons.

In Logistics, new terms have appeared like e-procurement, which refers to the purchase of materials, equipment, services and undertakings electronically. Supplier's catalogs appear on the screens of the company's employees, and items may be acquired with a simple click, without waste of time. It is a time when those who buy hold smaller stocks and those who sell do it with greater speed. Also, new competitors appear daily, upsetting acquired stabilities. In other words, there are no definite clients in this environment.

The emergence of e-commerce in sales of finished products has advanced new businesses, exposed the company to new clients, and placed products in places where, previously, companies had no access to. It has made production quickly sensitive to fluctuations and changes, each day in a less plannable way.

Furthermore, new software to monitor production and interconnect the e-connected client to the productive and logistic system constantly appears on the market. Marketplaces are more than just a virtual reality. They are in fact, a new market.

In this new market, corporations' internal systems move away from a collection of static interfaces to diversified applications, becoming ERPs type corporations (Figure 30). Some of these applications include those offered by companies such as SAP, ORACLE and so many others known worldwide.

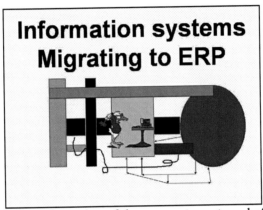

Figure 30 – Configuration of the corporate systems before ERP (Enterprise Resource Planning)

In e-procurement, progress relates to what Figure 31 illustrates. First come the telephone and fax; then come software solutions for process automation; and finally relationship marketplaces are created.

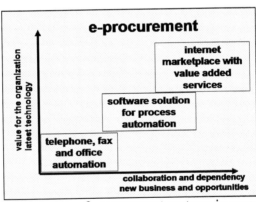

Figure 31 – Progress of procurement systems in organizations

Because the number of buyers and sellers vary, a strategy for purchase/sale may be established. This is what Figure 32 shows.

If there are few sellers and few buyers, a strategic and operational alliance may be indicated, depending on quality and support variables. If there are various buyers and only one seller, the model becomes seller-centric and offers special characteristics which you will explore, depending on whose side you are on.

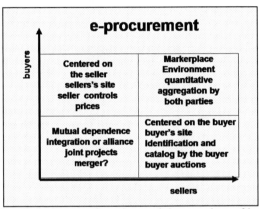

Figure 32 – Solutions as functions of the number of buyers and sellers

If there are many sellers and few buyers, the procurement model is indicated, because according to it, market approaches define the most attractive conditions for buyers. If, however, the market becomes elastic, with players on each side, the best alternative is the marketplace, where group purchasing techniques and other modalities to obtain the best price and delivery times from the market are used.

The opportunities in this area are many. One that has been highly used is reverse auctions, where buyers associate themselves and define, for a determined item, the maximum price they will pay, creating a strong competitive force in the supplier market and generating significant-discount prices. Large batches mutually attract small prices. And the price opportunity becomes an ever more frequent reality given the available means of communication.

But let's not waste our attention on a theme that has been well explored and for times with little depth. For example, solutions sellers commonly approach the reduction of prices by an increase in scale. However, several other aspects need to be analyzed when the issue is price reduction. Namely, how much discount is obtained; if the item has price elasticity; if we are dealing with a cartel, a monopoly, etc. The subject is vast and there are consultancies who sell sourcing on how to choose the best way to purchase groups of items, with pre-defined advantages.

To further develop the discussion of scale, elasticity and prices, Figure 33 shows how item B undergoes a large variation in prices with an increase in the quantity to be acquired. Or else, item B is sensitive to scale.

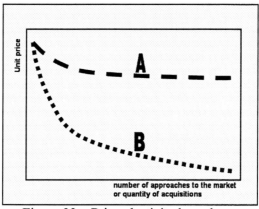

Figure 33 – Price elasticity by volume

Since item A is little influenced by scale, it has little sensitivity to quantity or number of market approaches. It may be a high market density item or even a monopoly or cartel.

Besides, theoretically, only the first approaches will provide the expected gains, because once an adjusted price has been reached, the next gains tend to be much less significant than the first ones, already obtained.

These aspects should be considered and thoroughly reviewed when defining a strategy to choose to further implement an e-solution model. Choices of portals, associations or integration of e-commerce or e-procurement companies should always be analyzed structurally and within a strategic long-term vision.

Because market changes happen with high speed, the time to make a decision may be more important than the technical accuracy of the evaluation (see Figure 34). Reaching high levels of accuracy may take a long time, since the more precision one seeks, the more time one spends to obtain an increase in information. In many cases, only part of the total information is enough for decision making, since the decision itself already involves a series of risks and uncertainties, inherent to the process of being distant from a future reality or from what is yet to happen.

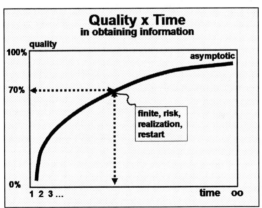

Figure 34 –Quality and time in information gathering

It's safe to say that 70% of good information comes within a time frame that allows it to influence decision making and allows actions and inevitable corrections to be anticipated according to prospective systems. By accumulating successive decisions, the theoretical design of Figure 35 would follow.

The decision may come in waves. In each round, 70% of the information is gathered, allowing us to make successive approximations to what is desired. Also, because there is time, the first visions can be put into practice soon, and successive restarts and complementations can be performed in the succeeding phases.

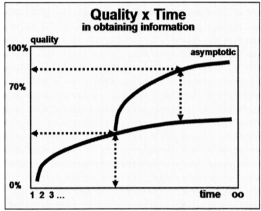

Figure 35 – Quality and time in information gathering:
Successive decisions and corrections

In each case, in a short time, sellers and buyers simultaneously perform the roles of allies and competitors, creating a new way of living in modern society (Figure 36). Although it brings conflicts, it also transforms these conflicts in great opportunities for co-constructing knowledge and shared cooperation.

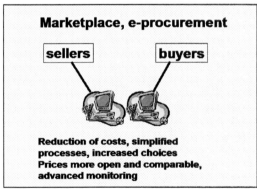

Figure 36 –Schematics of the marketplace

Thus, information systems are at the two nerve centers of the acquisition process: First it is at the internal integrated systems that allow less duplication of activities and ensure uniqueness of data in the system; second, it is at the external market vision, by means of portals and internet solutions, for the public and for providers.   They have changed the way of acquiring and delivering products and have affected Logistics in a direct and challenging way.

10 – Decentralizing and Sharing Services

A possible definition for the term "to decentralize" is "Whoever needs a resource to produce something should acquire it, with autonomy." The simplest level of productive organization considered and measured is the Business Unit, which should acquire the resources that it needs to make its products (resources may be understood as services, materials or information). After all, this Unit depends on them to meet the established results and survive. As such, it should have the autonomy to acquire it from whoever it is, for whichever price agreed, in the time it judges convenient, and within the ethical limits and practices acceptable to the environment. For example, based on Figure 37, units UO1, …UOn, AJ1, …AJn, WW1, …WWn use resources R1, R2, Rn. If they needed specific resources, which would be used in isolation, as for example R9, each unit should be able to acquire them autonomously.

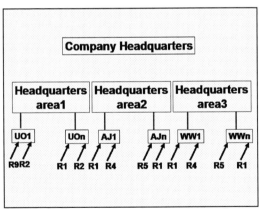

Figure 37- Organization, business units, and resources

If one or more units use common resources, for example R2, the units may share their acquisition, which would be performed by one of the players (a node in the logistics network) for all the others. The acquisition could also be performed by an immediately superior organizational level, if there are service contracts to regulate the interfaces. To acquire R2, which only exists in AREA 1 units, either UO1 acquires it for all, or UO2 acquires it for all, or the AREA 1 network acquires it, optimizing the acquisition of the resource. In the case of resource R1, common to UOs , AJs and ...WWs, more units are candidates to accomplish the acquisition. It may be that a unit from AJ, or UO , or WW executes it, or even the head office of the COMPANY in place of all of them. This view embraces the specifications of the item to acquire.

However, there is another approach, different from the previous and no less important, which does not deal with the specifications of the item to acquire, but with the similarity of the acquisition process. That is to say, all the items are R (resources) and are similarly obtained. Therefore, they may be acquired by service concentrators, despite of their specifications. This optimizes the acquisition process. In this case, besides service agreements, there is need of firming competence agreements, because acquiring resources differentially sophisticated may require a minimum knowledge of the composition of each resource, in addition to purchasing techniques. From the procurement point-of-view that prevails internationally, contracting services, purchases or resources for undertakings are conjugated activities comparable to 30% of the gross revenue of a productive segment, in average.

Acquiring resources entails attention to several variables that directly interfere with the profitability of the Business Units. They are response time, delivery time, processing costs, control of resource price, and evaluation of the intrinsic quality of the resource.

There is no fixed rule for decentralization, nor for sharing, but there are business results that should direct the actions of those who decide for maximum autonomy with multiplication of resources, or for maximum concentration / sharing with reduction of autonomy; or even for something hybrid, intermediate and intelligible that would provide sufficient negotiating autonomy for the independent units and the appropriate cost reduction by optimizing the acquisition process of resources which are common to all.

Lack of consistent service level agreements may undo the gains
from sharing. Lack of definition of responsibilities may inhibit
cost reduction. There are no extreme winners. In Figure 38, the
concave Total Cost curve represents the ideal total cost, taking
into account a good balance between AUTONOMY and
SHARING.

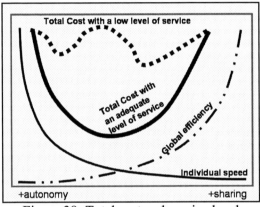

Figure 38- Total cost and service level

The concavity of the minimum value is lost in case perfect
service levels are not assured or the interface rules among
players are inefficient. If the objective function is
decentralization with sharing, restriction functions that limit
policy, regional, cultural and elasticity characteristics of the
supplier market are necessary for a model as close as possible to
the business reality of the moment to be reached. The search for
a solution for the set 'objective function and restriction
functions' leads to an optimum point between decentralizing
and sharing on one hand, and autonomy on the other. Anyway,
an explicit choice of focus should be made *a priori*, whether on
the specifications of the item or on the acquisition process.
The success of new organizations, be those that are freshly
beginning of those that resulted from transformations of other
previous existing companies, depends on factors such as service
innovation, support services and the ability to excel
expectations, costs-market compatibility, and aggressive use of
emerging technologies (e-procurement, e-commerce).

One of the well accepted models in new organizations are shared services that "sell" services to the business units with negotiated and established service levels, and prices and costs close to those of the market. These shared services are governed by relationship regulations duly documented and commonly entail the following activities: Finance, Human Resources, Information Technology, Environment, Health, Industrial Security, Materials Supply, and General Administration.

The rationale behind the existence of shared services is the economies of scale, because services are offered to multiple users and service levels and costs are controlled by the business areas.

It is necessary to clearly differentiate shared service activities from corporate activities (such as policies, strategies and guidance/evaluation), which are functions intrinsic to the top management of an organization or even of the business owners themselves. In both cases, people who require levels of control over the operations.

Thus, shared services should reduce costs (the service should cost less than if it were done by the business unit itself) while keeping the quality indexes of service supply high. Although they are not part of the corporation's core business, they should be approached as such and directed to the company's common processes. In some cases, they can supply services for third parties, pursuing cost sharing and taking advantage of the competences acquired.

Centralized or decentralized, hybrid, concentrated, nodes in the logistics network models, each cater to a specific moment and need of the organization. There is always a way of formatting ideas and channeling them into efforts toward increased productivity and reduced needs and performance demands.

To exemplify the idea, let's take a model of generic processes in the Logistics of Materials Supply (Figure 39). The model entails three processes:

- At the center is the flow of materials, where the treatment of use demand, acquisition and logistics begin, feeding use of and removing resources from the market;

- at the upper part is the optimization of supply logistics, which aims at the results of the business and deals with policies, strategies and evaluation of the system;
- at the bottom of Figure 39 is the infrastructure with specialties available for the whole system, from the treatment of issues related to material items and purchasing categories to the qualification of suppliers, maintenance of information systems, new logistical technologies, etc.

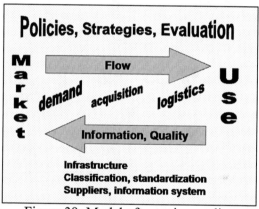

Figure 39- Model of generic supplies

Basically, the model tends to emphasize the role of advanced supplies, proactive in relation to the true demands of those who use materials and interactive in relation to the supplier market. Actually, it's a model that searches for the best mechanisms to supply the company's business, with maximum security and minimal loss and cost. Alliances, e-procurement and logistics vision are built-in to Sourcing. None of them is dispensable and all should receive appropriate treatment at the correct time, since these procedures are differentials in a competitive market. If they lack, unnecessary costs and insufficient speed in supply processing are generated.

The vision of the quality of materials and suppliers allows a rational and effective tracking of the life cycle of the material in its application. At the same time, this vision avoids the repetition of errors, assures that weights of good performance are considered in new purchases, and gives the user the capacity to complain, reject, and repair materials and equipment operational problems.

Organizations should balance well strategic, operational and control activities. They should not deal with these separate activities in a confused way. If they do so, they run the risk of losing the focus and efficiency (Figure 40):

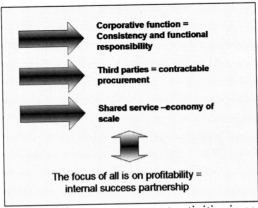

Figure 40- The different procurement activities in companies

The Supply Chain vision should prevail, involving all the players in the logistics cycle. The classic model includes Logistics, Acquisition and Operations.

Since Logistics fits the concept of services perfectly, it is in order to illustrate the difference between shared services and centralized systems. This is what Figure 41 does.

In centralized systems, the centralizer creates the strategy of the function, controls the resources and, classically, maintains the vision and the functional knowledge of the organization. In shared services, the Business Unit manager, or simply the user, creates the strategies, controls the resources, chooses and evaluates shared services.

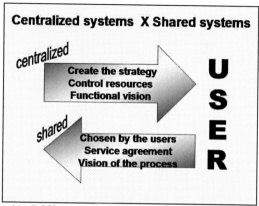

Figure 41- Different procurement activities in companies

The propelling vector of the movement changes direction in each one of the modalities cited. Even if the alternative chosen is not the most suitable for the environment, the following tenets should be bore in mind:

- it should be possible to return or migrate from one extreme to the other. That is, it should be possible to go from a shared system to a centralized one, or vice-versa, because new technologies, market pressures, times of crisis or mergers and incorporations may suggest the opposite modality as the best option;
- the "grey organizational zone" should not be allowed. It represents a doubtful system or a system with undefined responsibilities.   As such, it would subject the corporation to unnecessary power games and internal conflicts, generating loss of energy. In this respect, the organization should opt for one of the alternatives and convince its personnel that it is the best option for the moment, even though it knows that there are also advantages in the opposite modality.

11 –Total cost of Acquisitions

An input or resource for a productive process has the function of composing a product, which for its turn has a final market value. After this product is sold, whether it is goods or services, the value gives back to the producer some of the capacity to operate its new production and reinvest in improvements to the system. The value also helps producers to obtain profits (Figure 42).

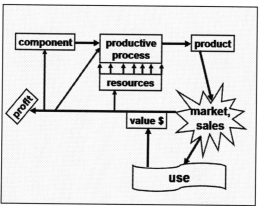

Figure 42 – Schematics for the realignment of value

Therefore, the best contribution of an input or resource is not its face value at the time of purchase, but its contribution and its cost in the productive process. When selecting an input or resource to purchase, which variables should be considered for comparison of value? Some possible variables are the following:

- price;
- delivery Period;
- quality;
- yield;
- useful life;
- information.

Thus, instead of buying (acquiring) an input or resource for the simple price for which it is offered, we could buy this very same production item, among various options in the supplier market, for its total cost in the productive process, where it will be applied later.

To do so, we need to identify the relevant variables for each productive system, since there may be differences between them. We need also to identify the separate weights for each variable. That is, the same input / resource may serve for two different productive processes, one that produces a product / final value of 10 and another that produces a product / final value of 100, with separate responsibilities and values for each process.

There is a series of acquired goods or equipments that are highly influenced by costs during their use or useful life. Yet, there are others that suffer little *a posteriori* influence on costs, or even have identical or very close costs for different specifications (Figure 43). In this case, as shown in figure 43, there is only the cost / purchase price, at time zero, because the future costs do not exist or are insignificant along the useful life of the input/resource. For example, a gold nugget, a precious stone, or a stand full of books.

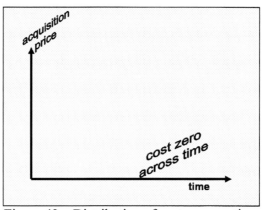

Figure 43 – Distribution of costs across time

In some other cases, as shown in Figure 44, even if costs incur across time, they will be identical or have the same order of magnitude. This would make it impossible to differentiate between the products in example A and those in B, as Figure 44 shows:

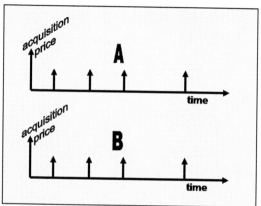

Figure 44 – Comparative costs for two series

Therefore, our special interest, first of all, rests on the identification of cases that contain the variables that influence the total cost, and on measuring the size of the differences.

Second, there is a strong interest in discovering the future costs in advance, in identifying and measuring these costs. We want to find out how precise and verifiable they are.

This interest derives from the unpredicabilities of the future. If we acquire something today, based on future costs calculated by expectations and predictions, we are dealing with an experiment after all, despite of how much scientific and verifiable the estimation is. This estimation defines an action and a decision in actual time (today), and we compute it without any possibility of verifying which will be the real facts or what will happen in the future.

In the case of Figure 45, products C and D hold distinct purchase prices and costs during their useful lives. This allows us to compare the total costs of the two series.

Among others, the most common factors that differentiate costs across the useful life of a production item are

- energy consumed;
- maintenance;
- spare parts;
- technical support;
- remaining value at the end of the life cycle;
- resale value;
- logistics (movement, transportation, stocks etc.).

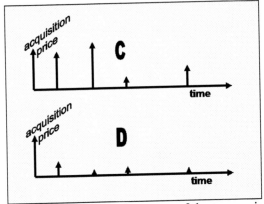

Figure 45 – Comparative costs of the two series and their differentials

Such an understanding becomes more visible in the acquisition of complex equipments that do not match standard specifications, but that are sensitive to specification and manufacturing processes with content, quality, and differentiated applications as functions of who supplies the manufacturers, how they use the supplies, among others.

Therefore, when these costs during the useful life of an equipment or input are significant, compared to its simple price at the time of purchase, an analysis of acquisitions by TCO (Total Cost of Ownership) becomes interesting. To apply the TCO systematics, other logistics and usage costs are taken into account too, besides price. The financial flow this schematics yields is presented in Figure 46.

That is, prices are situated at time zero and there are a series of other costs that are identifiable and measurable, which are also significant price wise.

To reach the TCO, all the values of each position should be loaded to zero time, coinciding with the price, taking into account the interest rate and time. This yields a single value that represents the whole flow, which should then be compared with other alternative solution flows under study. Such mechanism is known as the NPV system (Net Present Value).

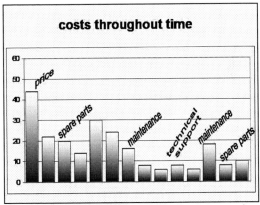

Figure 46 – Specifications of costs across time

Therefore, to purchase for the total cost means not to buy for the simple purchase price only, but to take into account future costs and load them to the purchase price. This gives us a single value that conjugates price and costs and that directs the decision according to all costs involved and not just the purchase price.

Example:

A company wants to buy microcomputers within the TCO view. For it to do so, it needs to consider the following variables:

- Installation cost;
- Maintenance costs;

- Response time for repairs;
- Quantity of bundled software;
- Throwaway cost (disposal).

Supposing three proposals from different suppliers have been received, the following table could be put together:

Supplier	A	B	C
Purchase price	2500	2700	3100
Installation Cost	100	90	110
Maintenance cost per month	10	10	9
Response time for repairs	6 hours	4 hours	3 hours
Quantity of bundled software	3	5	9
Disposal cost	110	70	0

Consider yet:

36 months of use;
Cost of production stoppage per hour = 100;
Number of estimated stoppages in 36 months = 3;
Price of additional software = 100;
Monthly interest rate = 1%.

For the specific case of computers, there are some frequent questions which lead to the use of Total Cost of Acquisition, since they sensibly influence the use of this mechanism. The questions are

- How is the equipment updated?
- What are the costs and unavailabilities at the time of uninstallation?
- What are the risks of undue use of information or insertion of technologies in unused equipments?
- What will be the equipment destination when discarded in the environment?
- What is its maximum residual value for re-utilization?

- How much does the administration of multiple points and remote points cost?

Figure 47 shows a U-shaped curve or a basin graph, which represents a region with problems and adjustment deviations at the beginning; a region of normality and productivity at the center; and, at the end, deviations start again until the end of the equipment useful time, when the viability of replacement and renovation begins to be calculated.

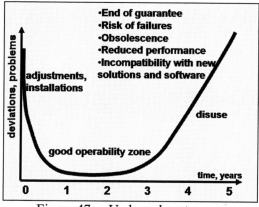

Figure 47:   U-shaped cost curve

This graph and these concepts are valid for a large quantity of equipment and systems, not only computers. They could be used for rotating equipment (pumps, turbines, compressors etc.), elements which have wear and tear and performance (vehicles), among many other groups of goods in use.

What is the proposed solution?
By taking time from 1 to 36 months (since the cost of maintenance is 10 monetary units per month), the following table can be produced:

time	Monthly Value	Moved Value (time zero)	interest 1
0	0	0.0	
1	10	9.90	
2	10	9.80	
3	10	9.71	
4	10	9.61	
5	10	9.51	
6	10	9.42	
7	10	9.33	
8	10	9.23	
9	10	9.14	
...	...	...	
36	10	6.99	

To compute each value of the moved value column (time zero) the following steps should be taken:

$$\text{moved value} = \frac{10}{(1+\text{interest}/100)^{\text{time}}}$$

This table shows the weights for the monthly maintenance value of 10, at 1% interest, over 36 months.
If each value of 10 is brought to time zero, and the new series is accumulated, the representative value of 301.08 is obtained.
The more distant from time zero, the less influential the monthly value of 10 becomes. Note that at time 36, the value 10 becomes 6.99, while at time 1 it is worth 9.90.
Now a cash flow can be designed, taking into account the types of costs and their applications across time:

Supplier	A	B	C
Price	2500	2700	3100
Installation costs	100	90	110
Maintenance costs	301	301	271

Cost of stoppages	1800	1200	900
Quantity of bundled software	600	400	0
Throwaway cost	110	70	0
Total cost	5411	4761	4381

Within the view provided by such reasoning, the best option is from supplier C, even though it quotes a higher initial price.

Part of this reasoning involves subjectivity because it spreads relative costs according to future expectations. The decision-making body of the company should debate and accept them internally. Although decision-making under such conditions may not be completely comfortable, it can reduce final costs and increase the corporation's profits.

A rather normal practice is to do a history survey for each supplier and their performance with other clients. The values obtained support decisions about future variables. We should not forget that we are dealing with a probabilistic approach, which involves uncertainties and predictions and should be treated as such.

The following table presents a comparison of the percentages for each cost by the total cost:

Supplier	A	%A	B	%B	C	%C
Price	2500	46	2700	57	3100	71
Installation cost	100	2	90	2	110	3
Maintenance costs	301	6	301	6	271	6
Cost of stoppage	1800	33	1200	25	900	21
Quantity bundled software	600	11	400	8	0	0
Disposal cost	110	2	70	1	0	0
Total cost	5411	100	4761	100	4381	100

Note that supplier C shows the greatest proportional cost at time zero, showing lower percentage costs across time.

Probably, it is a more sophisticated equipment that offers more benefits. Only with use and over time can these benefits be verified. If it were to be bought just for its simple price, it would never be acquired.

To implement a system of total cost of acquisition, you should follow the sequence of events below:

1. identify the 5 items most sensitive to the application of total cost evaluation (that is, items for which the prices are not the only factor in deciding a purchase);
2. analyze the acquisition practices for the selected items in other companies, within the country and overseas;
3. identify the main cost variables used for the selected items;
4. obtain the average percentage values of each variable in relation to their total cost of acquisition;
5. create a matrix with the main variables and the average values used to choose acceptable average percentage values for the cost variables. Then use these average percentages to make an acquisition decision;
6. create a contract for the acquisition and for managing its use over time. That is, spreading payments, evaluation mechanisms, payment release procedures, efficiency clauses, and penalties across time of use.

Let's introduce another example related to the acquisition of chemical products for industrial processes:
A given industrial process uses a whitener which is mixed with the final product in sufficient quantities to reach a certain standard. Two manufacturers of the whitener have been registered. Their products have distinct characteristics. Here is the data for each one.

	Type A	Type B
Volume of whitener per volume of the final product m^3/m^3	0.05	0.07
Purchase logistics $/m^3$	0.8	0.5
Throwaway logistics of plastic drums $/m^3$	0.3	0.4
Tests / m^3 of the product $	0.02	0.01

For what quantities is type A more economical than type B?

To reach a solution, the same reasoning steps used in the previous example should be taken. Use the current value to load each cost to time zero and then compare them.

In other words, resort to Total Cost of Acquisition procedures. They require:

- Standardization of processes and products;
- Inclusion of products and correlated sequences (do not use a part of a process or product that comprises other parts);
- Serious and abundant documentation (lack of data distorts and invert decisions);
- Recordings of the progress and corrections allowed;
- Wholesale or batch purchases.

They also require that a general cost structure be applied. One possible suggestion would be the following:

Research
        Concepts
        Viability
        Market evaluation
        Basic documentation

Development
        Detailed evaluation
        Quantification
        Models
        Prototypes
        Pilot
        Project
        Tests

Investment
        Acquisitions
        Fabrication
        Management

Construction
Assembly
Operational tests
Specific logistics
Installations
Tests of operation
Supervision and pre-operation

Operations
Personnel
Consumable materials
Energy
Availability
Redundancy
Contingency
Training
Inspection

Maintenance
Preventive
Predictive
Corrective
Parts and pieces
Consumable materials
Qualified Personnel

Disposal
Environment
Replacement
Resale value

This list is not complete, but is the logical structure for a general case of a system submitted to analysis within the Total Cost of Acquisition vision. Each situation should be analyzed and dissected with its real current variables. The objective is to capture all the involved component parts of cost and thus allow the present value of a series of costs to represent, by means of a single value, the sum total of the project as a whole.

12 - Lognormal and selective usage of a third party

By observing the disposition of nature's elements, we can retrieve a model (naturally, a reductionism that focuses on our field of interest only), for the distribution of large events that occur in small quantities (or low frequencies) and for small events that occur in large quantities (or high frequencies).

Figure 48 explains this distribution. The largest circle, above and to the left, is isolated, because it represents the largest event and occurs with the lowest frequency. The circles to the right and below represent events that occur with the highest frequencies and consequently show the smallest sizes. This is also true of nature: Rains are more frequent than floods, because they have reduced sizes and impacts. Floods have bigger sizes and impacts, therefore they occur less frequently.

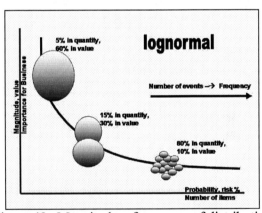

Figure 48 –Magnitude x frequency of distribution

Projecting this understanding to the material or service domain, the following examples could be given:

1 – If we kindly ask our housekeeper to buy mayonnaise for the weekend, s/he would go to the closest supermarket and buy 3 or 4 bottles of mayonnaise of a given brand. For that purpose, we could leave a dozen or so dollars. After the purchase, the housekeeper would put the products away in the pantry, leave the change on the table, and we would close the matter. The

brand is not so important. The only aspect that should be verified is the date of validity.

2 – Now, if we are to buy a car, we could not do it like in the case of the mayonnaise. An analysis of prices, insurance costs, annual license fee , maintenance costs, miles per gallon, value of the automobile after 2-3 years, other information from friends who use the same model, a little bit of emotion (since no one is made of steel), and the choice is finally made. The matter is solved. The person signs a check, pays for the car, and at the most, the personal driver would go to the dealer to get the car and drive it home to park it in the garage.

3 – And what about an apartment or house? Well, this would take us at least three months. We would have to analyze and check everything, from the plans & blueprints of the house to the materials used, the neighborhood, the distance from work, schools, shops, the position of the sun, its value, property taxes, insurance, nearest public transportation stations, friends' houses and much more. We would not ask a third party to make even the payment. We would take the day off to pay and sign the papers personally.

Or else, the way we acquire items correlates to the items' value or importance.

Going back to the context of goods and services, companies accomplish acquisitions in the same way. Simple items, of little value, of generic use, are frequently bought. They may be third partied, with control.

Medium-sized items are partially acquired by third parties. However, the essence of the acquisition (the choice, the specification, and the authorization to buy) is made by the owner of the asset.

Large-sized items, with high values, are always acquired by the owner, never by third parties. The owner does it all, or almost all.

This is the meaning of the ABC lognormal graph (Figure 48): The set of acquisitions should be seen according to the dimensions frequency, value, and importance.

This view, associated with the view of complexity *versus* criticality, form the basis of a strategic vision for acquisitions. The stratification of the approach is fundamental. Top management should take care of large acquisitions, without neglecting the medium and never abandoning control of the small ones.

To acquire does not mean just to purchase, but to internalize a resource in a complete manner, guaranteeing its performance in the main productive process, contemplating needs such as parts, pieces, maintenance, support, stocks, control of consumables, life cycle, payment and, finally, resale or disposal.

Let's take another example. An airplane assembly company will acquire turbines with the total participation of the upper management (similarly to what happened with the above described items A). Perhaps, because the airplane tires do not have the same level of attractiveness, they will not be acquired in the same way the turbines were, but with less participation of the upper management. Also, very probably, the curtains and the seats will not be acquired in the same way as the turbines either.

The decision mechanisms on these matters involve questions about:

- Alternatives and risks;
- Expectations and future vision;
- Preferences and personal-related aspects in the decisions;
- Consequences, damages, destination of the profits.

The purpose and importance of this characterization is twofold. First, it allows the evaluation of strategic actions and not of sequenced operational ones. Second, it develops understanding of these actions. If non-trivial actions are implemented, and they sometimes do not belong to common sense, care, communication and special training are required. Without these, there may be divergence among the strategies and operational variables.

It follows that acquisition personnel (purchases and contractions) should be organized according to the different actions necessary for each group of materials or services. The profile of personnel who take care of items A should be distinct from that of those who work with items B and C. Qualification, and time to dedicate to each matter should be considered in establishing responsibilities and all should collude to attribute value to the analyses of items A.

In Logistics, the relativity of size, independently of the variable under analysis, suggests differentiated treatments. This is to say that a few very large projects are treated differently from many small projects, even if they are of a similar nature. In one more instance, let's take the case of systematic transportation of large cargos and the repeated transportation of small cargos. They would have fundamentally different treatments. A transporter of large turbines (36-feet long, 40-inches thick) act and plan differently from transporters of radio batteries or cans of milk powder do, for example.

Obviously, various variables get into this reasoning, such as types and quantities of origins, types and quantities of destinations, geography, routes, payment types and remuneration, buyer and seller profiles, among others. Figure 49 illustrates this reasoning. The vertical axis represents the dimension "size" or the value of importance of a given variable.

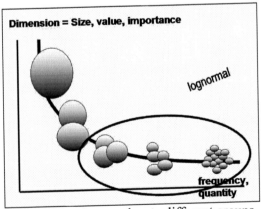

Figure 49 – Approaches to different groups

For example, weight to be transported, volume to be lifted, distance to be run etc. The horizontal axis represents the frequency, the repetition, the number of events for each dimension; that is, how much transportation is done at the time unit considered; how many volumes are carried; how many times the same distance will be covered, etc.

Therefore, given a set of logistics activities from a productive process, whether manufacturing of items or supply of services, it is possible to design a lognormal graph for a stated reality or even for a projected one.

In another example, let's suppose a transporter is invited to transport goods from a liquid packager (soft drinks), from Houston to New Orleans, with the following predicted demand per week:

WEEK	20 liter drums	SOURCES	2 liter bottles	SOURCES	350 ml bottles	SOURCES
1	100	2	4000	5	100000	22
2	110	2	3800	5	95000	22
3	110	2	4000	6	100000	22
4	110	2	4200	6	100000	20
5	100	2	4300	6	110000	23
6	90	1	4400	7	110000	24
7	90	1	4500	7	120000	24

Given the small variations predicted, it is not necessary to calculate the averages and standard deviations. We can use approximate numbers, typical of estimates.

Again, we will see that large volumes associate with high frequencies in an intuitive manner, while high frequencies correlate with small unit volumes. Also, captation occurs in larger quantities for small volumes as would be equally probable to occur with destinations.

Thus, the treatment of large-low-frequency volumes is different from the one dispensed to small-high-frequency volumes. The large ones have a more individual treatment, per project, because they are repeated less, are rarer, while the small volumes are frequent, showing significant repetition.

The small-high-frequency volumes tend to be dealt with by consolidation, by management of continuity, with diluted costs and frequent contingencies.

On the other hand, large-scale, less-frequent events have a more individual, personalized treatment, with fewer contingencies (even though contingencies are always equally possible). For this group, each event enjoys high relevance and may be dealt with as if it were a different project.

Practically, the two groups have distinct management variables. Because of response characteristics, demand requirements, resource specifications, it is normal to have different personnel taking care of each group.

Thus, many logistics processes may be segregated into personnel groups with distinct approaches, as a function of their characteristics and demands. Because I intended to reach a broad application when writing the book, the textual examples are generic and do not restrict any view.

In brief, logistics issues related to large and rare events as opposed to frequent and small ones should be approached differently. If we borrow concepts from the Natural Sciences, which use nature itself to conceive rules of study, we see that in all these matters there are two separate phases: EXPLORATION and EXPLOITATION. Exploration deals with research, analysis, modeling, conception. Exploitation deals with production, efficiency, implementation, and execution. A well conducted exploratory phase allows quality selection. It is possible to choose from one group and from what is complementary to it; to see what is relatively important and what may be dealt with in consolidation groups, without neglecting the business characteristics. Exploitation, or the phase of implementation, should follow the suggested exploratory model, allowing new explorations to be fed in systematically.

The exploratory phase goes from the correct understanding of the data, to the perception of what the company's logistical situation and characteristics are, up to the adoption of the best logistics models available.

These two terms, exploration and exploitation, represent the relative irreversibility of some actions in Logistics. Part of the definitions and decisions in Logistics cannot be retaken. Consequently, a robust, well-discussed model tends to be better implemented than one that bears a simple division into groups of materials or services, according to experimental variables. Some algorithms, some logics in the selection of the sets are necessary. Only then will we achieve distinct and controlled treatments for specific contexts.

13 - Standardization

There are at least three different types of standardizations in industrial productive environments, which are

- specifications or technical;
- procedural;
- documental.

Within the first group of "standardizable processes" are definitions of materials, equipment and services that represent a range of options and reduce the quantity of alternative specifications. In it you will find studies of the supplier market capacity and of how to reduce the quantity of specification ranges.

For example, imagine the use of metallic tubes which vary from 2 to 40 inches in diameter, in various internal corporation applications. Instead of using any diameter calculated as a specification for purchase, the designer opts for diameters which fall into representative ranges. Therefore, the standards could be 6, 10, 14, 18, 22, 26, 30, 34, and 40. In case the calculations indicated a diameter of 13.4, the design would be recalculated for 10 and 14 and one of these possibilities would be chosen unless there were insuperable technical restrictions.

Consequently, the whole system--which uses the tubes and invests in them-- benefits from this standard choice, which involves fewer applied specifications, lower stocks for updating, lower quantity of maintenance tools, greater sharing of parts and supplementary pieces among others.

On the supplier market side, prices get lower too, because machines and processes are better setup, manufacturing processes and tool racks are optimized, and availability times are quicker, among other things.

The second group of "standardizable processes" is a set of procedures, that is, ways in which we obtain goods and services in the market. Because an item does not exist by itself or its intrinsic specifications, different organizations may differ in the way they approach the acquisition of the same equipment. The approach will depend on how the equipment relates to the productive chain that it will serve. Suppliers are chosen, orders are proposed, prices are compared, manufacturers are chosen, services and parts are incorporated, much more as functions of the complexity of the supplier market and the criticality of the application than of any other factor. Each situation has a standard procedure or recommendation. The procedures should set bounds for attitudes, times, phases, levels of competence, and controls.

The third group of "standarizable processes" involves the company documentation at its various levels. Within this group are issues related to the selection of types of documents (reserved, confidential, secret, internal distribution, external distribution), groups by functions (purchases, sales, accounting, financial, engineering, maintenance, Logistics), format (only paper, only electronic), backups, physical redundancy etc.

Sizes, logos, font sizes, standardization of signatures, the position of each of the contents within each document, dates, optical recognition, tracking, exchanges with external environments (with suppliers, consumers and service suppliers), and all aspects related to the issuing and reception of documents in a company may be grouped into minimum standards. They will significantly facilitate retrieval, speed of interpretation, reduction of errors, and controls. Rewriting, re-registration, duplication of an act should also be observed and justify a reduction calculated by documental standardization.

To standardize means to normalize, reduce, schematize, bringing about all mechanisms of economy and reduction of dispersion and causing less errors and deviations. In brief, standardization

- creates consistency in a family of products;
- generates a repository of directives and standards;
- allows training of new users;
- improves the work of groups and teams;
- reduces errors;

- increases confidence;
- increases efficiency;
- reduces reinvention;
- reduces decisions without rules;
- reduces lead times, development and implementation of projects;
- facilitates re-utilization;
- facilitates interoperability among systems, units and separate areas.

These are the main benefits of standardizations.

To prepare standards and ensure that they are used, the main requirements are

- support from upper management;
- simplicity;
- wide participation in its conception;
- easy and intuitive communications;
- penalties for uses outside the standard, when there are no justifications;
- brief texts that go straight to the point;
- prizes, incentives;
- demonstrations of the advantages in simple language.

14 – Acquisition models

The attributions of an acquisitions department are, among others, the following:

To purchase:

- With technical quality;
- In the right quantity;
- At the right times;
- At a fair price;
- From a suitable supplier;
- With the best coupled services;
- For the right locale;
- Executing from procurement to payment.

There are various ways to acquire goods or services from the supplier market. For example, by:

- A. comparing prices for a given specification;
- B. weighting technical proposals in relation to prices;
- C. making a purely technical choice;
- D. examining the technological developments;
- E. developing alternative suppliers;
- F. making partnerships, alliances or contracts with special clauses;
- G. making third partied purchases;
- H. using reverse auctions.

Each one of them has its own most appropriate application. In some cases, more than one way may be suitable. The choice then will be made by pure intuition, previous experience or based on suggestion from others.

A – Comparing prices for a given specification
When the specification is firm, variations are not possible. In acquisitions of standardized goods or services from the market,

this alternative is well accepted. This is the case of acquisitions from distributors who buy from large worldwide manufacturers, as for example distributors of ordinary electric batteries.

In these cases, all the concern falls over conservation aspects, validity, origin, legality of the product. In theory, no special attention is given to variations in the specifications. Naturally, brands with notoriously low qualification are eliminated. It would be something like buying 100 batteries from Sanyo, Panasonic or Duracell. Since they are equivalent in quality and duration, their acquisition would require only a comparison of prices. Therefore, we are simply comparing prices for the same specifications.

Consequently, we can say that there are three parts in such an acquisition:

- Technical specifications or requirements;
- Prices;
- Financiability.

These three parts should not be mixed. Each one has its own time and is independent. First, prices for a given specification should be obtained, and then their financial aspects should be compared. If these independent steps are mixed, we run the chance of not understanding what is being counterbalanced to obtain lower prices. It is current practice to call for financial bids, once prices have been obtained.

The application of the lowest price is only possible broadly speaking or if it were possible to have completely equal objects. Something that is obviously not possible.

B – Weighting technical proposals in relation to prices
In the purchase of items manufactured according to tailored specifications that may vary in concentration, weight, volume or even performance, it is normal to relate prices to expected results, by using weighted factors.

Even if Total Cost of Acquisition is not used, weighted factors allow us to consider product variables and application variations, counterbalanced by prices.

Taking our previous example on the acquisition of a chemical whitener (page 93), it involved 2 products: Product A, with an efficiency of 1 liter per m^2 ; and product B, with an efficiency of 2 liters per m^2.

Well, putting aside factors such as logistics, storage, and handling, among others, and considering just efficiency as a factor, it would be reasonable to pay up to twice the price for product A. The logical reasoning is simple: Product A would take half of the final volume to process the very same area.

C – Making purely technical choices

There are cases for which a given demand requires a unique specification. In addition, in some cases this specification selects a single supplier because of its unique characteristics or even because it would be highly expensive to develop a new supplier.

In these cases, we are left with only one option: to conduct a skillful negotiation that envisions long term contracts and clauses of logistics efficiency and price reduction per volume, among others.

A word of caution is in order. The dependence of an entire productive process on a single product or single supplier requires stocked contingency volumes for crises and continuous analyses of alternatives.

D – Examining technological developments

Productive processes systematically require new technological levels that are not available in natural approaches to the market. This gives room for technological development. There are various names for this mechanism, for example, Technological Agreements, Terms of Cooperation, Technological Development, among others.

The essence of an agreement of this nature is a special contract for collaborative development, in which the requester and the developer open specifications, resources, share restricted information, coordinate multidisciplinary teams and reach levels of greater applicability than those present in the conventional market. The product may be a prototype or a first production piece, and the acquisition should contemplate a longer relationship between the parties, which assures future acquisitions for an agreed period of time.

E – Developing alternative suppliers

To have only one supplier of a material or service is not very much recommended. Companies are disqualified or sold and may even disappear. In other words, if you only have one, you might have none.

Therefore, developing alternative suppliers is important to undo a dependency or even obtain better prices, generating competition.

Obviously, this action should be clearly defined in cases for which joint development strategies or long term contracts have been established because the intention is not to develop alternatives.

There are various ways of developing alternative suppliers. One of them is to check who supplies the main competitor. There are search methodologies or "sourcings" that are largely used for more complex and specific markets.

F – Making partnerships, alliances or contracts with special clauses

Partnerships and alliances are contracts between two institutions that share the same objective and similar products; both are parts of the companies' social missions.

If the agreement is between suppliers and clients, they are not denominated partnerships or alliances, but contracts with special clauses (including terms, logistics etc.). The clauses most commonly used are the logistics clauses (stocks, availabilities, package returns), or performance clauses (division of profits by reduction in times, elimination of number of errors etc.).

For example, in the purchase of equipments or pieces with immediate delivery times and stocks held by the supplier, a special contract between two parties, aiming at common gains, is typically signed, even though the parties' objects of survival are different. While the client supplies and shows its consumption data, variability, specifications, the supplier shows its times for manufacturing, transportation, etc.

G – Making third party purchases
Third party purchases are a mechanism to transfer activities and responsibilities to a third party or contractor (a contracted private person or company). The third party executes acquisitions in the name of the company or even in its own name, with the concomitant transference of power and property. Third party purchases may take into account price goals and price reductions and include the sharing of the advantages obtained.
This set entails the acquisitions by assemblers or integrators, also called EPC companies (Engineering, Procurement and Construction). They acquire equipment and parts and assemble the final set, system or even a complete productive unit.

H – Using reverse auctions
Reverse Auctions are a mechanism of obtaining lower prices in cycles, until a unique minimum value is reached. The supplier companies exercise the right to bid ever lower prices, up to their limits, until the last bid is given and no one else is able to reduce their prices. The last lowest bid is the winner.
This practice is suitable for stock materials and firm specifications that are not susceptible to manipulation, dilution or adulteration. In principle, it does not apply to engineered materials, because they are not made as alternatives for a firm, standard specification.

There are tools and associated dynamics, such as electronic purchases, direct purchases for the lower price, reverse auctions (the dynamics of price bidding until the lowest minimum final bid is submitted) etc. Such tools should be carefully applied, seeking not to destroy the local market, degenerate the specifications, or bring to bear impracticable prices. An understanding of all the factors and of the strategy precedes the choice of the acquisition mechanism.

Therefore, there are many available acquisition and contract models. Each market and moment requires a specific analysis of the acquisition models that best serve the objective of those who buy and of conserving the market for future negotiations. The modality that best responds to the set of selection questions should be chosen. Each case calls for reflection and a specific strategy and negotiation.

To be able to use a competitive environment, the technical specifications should balance the number of suppliers and the quality required. Excessive requirements may lead to choosing a brand, which, if necessary, should be made explicitly. To avoid eliminating competition, too rigorous requirements should be avoided too.

Figure 50 shows how to use average requirements to keep a number of suppliers that sustains competition, in cases where a pure technical choice is not the appropriate modality.

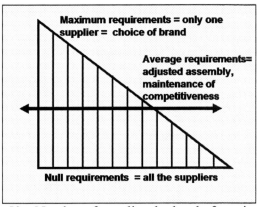

Figure 50 – Number of suppliers by level of requirements

15 - Prices of acquisitions and services

Acquisitions of goods and services form a significant part of the logistics vision. Each cent saved in the task of acquiring items becomes corporative profits.

To acquire means to obtain, incorporate a good or service fully. This includes transportation, taxes and all other aspects necessary to make the good available for use or to execute the service to add the designated value to the corresponding asset.

In organizations, three types of acquisitions are common. Namely:

- Goods;
- Pure services;
- Construction and assembly (when there are goods to be delivered at the end of the service).

Each one has its own singular, special characteristics and they should be explored.

In the case of goods acquisition, the vision of manufacturing qualification, adherence to specifications, value paid, delivery time, post- purchase support, spare parts, and value at the end of the life cycle should be kept under the focus of attention.

In the case of pure services acquisition, the relevant issues include manpower qualification, management of resources, chronograms, little interference in the productive system under development, Health, Security and Environment.

Construction and assembly, for its turn, represent the sum total of the two previous cases, that is, goods plus pure services. It combines manufacturing and services and as such demand attention to every previous aspect underlined.

To launch an acquisition process, three price referentials are commonly used:

- Historical reference;
- Market comparisons;
- Analytical construction of costs.

Historical references have their limitations, such as currency devaluations, technological changes, market adjustments, logistics modalities (INCOTERMS). However they may serve to verify tendencies, analyze deviations, existing coincidences with measurable variables (tubes related to steel, for example). It is not a sufficient method in itself, demanding other approaches.

However, it is a highly used method and offers interesting negotiation mechanisms if the due caution is taken--comparable specifications are used and possible variations are eliminated (currency changes, increases in price of spare parts, taxes, logistics etc.). With the due care, it can become a good tool for a first approach to the market, and when there are no other relevant facts that explain cost increases, historical references may serve for effective negotiation.

We should not forget that there are correction indexes available from federal agencies, other institutions and magazines specialized in economic analyses.

On the other hand, a market comparison comes in handy as a price referential, because it eliminates problems present in the first methodology (historical references). How does it do so? By searching for the values attributed to the desired acquisition item in the supplier market itself. Unfortunately, not always can it be executed. The reasons vary: Sometimes because the specifications are not standard; others because the market suppliers who are consulted are themselves interested in supplying that specific item. These facts may distort or even contaminate the information.

Comparisons of prices seem much more efficient in cases that get quotes for off-the-shelf items sold by one party and manufactured by another (sellers, the last interface before the end consumer, constitute a different party from manufacturers). The sellers cannot interfere in the specification or production costs / profits, but only in the costs of distribution and resale. In these cases, market comparisons are efficient and can be facilitated by specific available sites on the web that provide such a service and allow a first comparison.

Comparisons should be run not only among prices to be paid for a product, but on other possible costs, had them been inserted initially or not. For example, taxes, logistics (delivery), technical support, guarantee, replacement in case of failure, spare parts, repairs etc.

The analytical construction of costs is considered a robust tool, because it considers the sum of the costs of the parts, for what they are worth or cost, and yields a price composition. It consists of finding out how much each part costs and summing the costs up to attain a final composite value. There are limitations to this case too, because not all parts belong to public knowledge. Sometimes, even specialists do not know them. Therefore, it may not be simple to value each part. In addition, not always the manufacturing methods or source of the parts is fully known, making it difficult to reach a final composite value or even distorting it.

The cost analysis method is widely used by large corporations, and personnel who work in this area are normally specialized, having worked in operations or investments. They carry their real experiences over to the study and analysis of price referentials. A planned rotation of personnel is recommended, as well as care not to forget history and avoid repeating past errors. The process is cumulative, because experience is substantial.

When the prices are of a significant size for the business, a good technique consists of using the three approaches to price referentials simultaneously, that is, taking into account the three price vectors and comparing them. Thus, to precify or budget for means previously obtaining the most probable price to be reached, allowing the buyer or negotiator to make a secure and efficient negotiation. Figure 51 summarizes the vision of price referentials described.

Finally, it is worth remembering that upstream prices become costs along the processes, and prices in current processes become costs in downstream processes. That is, given the nature of the material or service, there are cumulative chains of profits, taxes, and logistics, besides the main intrinsic parts that constitute costs.

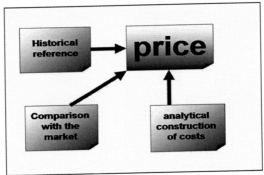

Figure 51 – The three price vectors

16 – Upstream engineering

Deviations along the route of a project are normal and necessary. These route corrections are more efficient and less costly when they occur further upstream from the process in progress, before the accomplishment of more stages. The earliest, the better.

This means that planning and discussing thoroughly before the start of the implementation reduces costs and losses, and avoids risks and postponements.

This concept is particularly true in procurement when thinking of standardization, market, and price analyses. With strategy and planning these activities naturally bring fewer risks.

Almost every human activity that is well planned has better chances of achieving success. For this purpose, planning needs to be understood as preparing future stages in advance, providing actions against surprises, preparing yourself, training, preparing for contingencies, and providing redundancy.

The generic graph in Figure 52 shows, in value, the comparative advantages of implementing changes or route deviations earlier. Why is it so? Because each moment that goes by means the execution and implementation of one more phase. If a phase is implemented and needs to be undone or redone, there is loss of time and values for the process.

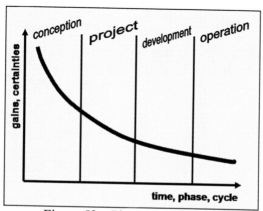

Figure 52 – Phases of a system

If this concept is applied to procurement, for example, it allows us to see that when an estimated price is not well defined, after market prices had been collected, there will be doubts about the capacity of the first-placed supplier to execute the services fully Wouldn't it be undersized for what it will be obliged to do? Or yet, wouldn't it have quoted an exaggerated price or even hindered a healthy and efficient negotiation because of a lack of consistent references? Such quality gaps may cause errors such as the declassification of suppliers and the need to hold new auctions for the same item.

These errors derive from doubts about just one estimated price.

Likewise, in an engineering project, the construction of a large operation unit may require reconstructions, dismounting and redesigning, if the project is not robust and detailed enough to avoid them. This would cause loss of lead times and direct values, as well as inevitable waste and friction between suppliers and contractors.

Total Cost of Acquisition is a clear example of how to apply future costs to planning. By using it, we can predict, as much as possible and in advance, what are the future costs of acquiring an item. This allows us to make current decisions based on the future. In case acquisitions do not occur by their total cost, we run the chance of discovering new and unexpected costs while we are in the process of using the items. Such a finding would distort previously taken decisions.

One of the most interesting sales secrets can be found in the upstream: Intense engineering loads cause conceptual purchases. This means that strategic companies assemble sales teams with highly qualified personnel, professionally and personally, in such a way that they live constantly with the opinion formers of the client company.

These opinion formers feed them in, both explicitly and subliminally, with ideas, innovations, concepts and values about the supplier company's products.

In other words, those who are influenced will continuously consider the information collected, automatically, when determining their specifications, projects, and price definitions.

To sell ideas might be more advantageous than to sell products, because it consolidates the very way of thinking of those who sells them and places the reason for the choice or preference on the words of those who specify.

17 - USER CHAIN

The efforts to move goods and provide services from the point of raw material to their application in a productive process and disposal after their useful life have always challenged logistics managers and systems. Such efforts have given rise to strategic concepts, approaches and management systems that have evolved over time. An important conceptual movement emerged with the appearance of INTEGRATED LOGISTICS. Integrated Logistics sought to align all the logistics segments of a given system with common bases. Later, another concept dominated the field: SUPPLY CHAIN, which included the suppliers and sub-suppliers, in a complex and realistic sequence that increased the capacity to rationalize supply actions for the productive chain. Therefore the SUPPLY CHAIN deals with the chain of supplies, pushing the system to the user's side. Until then, the focus was on productive systems and on the management of resources in an attempt to maximize the results of the supply chain in terms of the basic objectives in desired price, delivery, and quality

We find, however, that the onset of the supply spectrum begins with the end user himself. The users apply the goods or services produced or provided to their consumption or productive processes. They have habits, perceptions and feelings. Their demands are what actually determine the complex chain which makes products available and ultimately meet their needs. An important equalizer of such chains are the various players in the complete value chain, who interact with each other, and have interfaces with greater or lesser elasticity and power to absorb variations. Objectives, perceptions and vision may therefore be placed at opposite sides of the chain. The result: the system is conceived as a Pull instead of a Push model.

The cycle of use including the demand of those who use have the greatest equalizing force on the entire chain, hence the USER CHAIN evolves (Figure 53). It is from the demand for usage that the need for innovation, timely replacement, repetition of consumption and propagation of satisfaction information on products or services as well as on their disuse, re-use and disposal arose. These players who use, pay, expand and inform, should be active agents in the entire cycle; committed not only with their right to use what they pay for, but with their rights and obligations to define characteristics and functionalities: what, how, and in which ways their products and services should be not only supplied, but also produced, transported and even discarded.

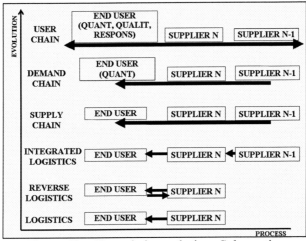

Figure 53 – User chain evolution: Schematics

As an evolution that started with Logistics and passed by Integrated Logistics, Reverse Logistics, Supply Chain, Value Chain, and Demand Chain, the end user must have total vision and influence on:

- Social responsibility (against child labor or slave workforce)
- Environment preservation as a whole
- Safety, personal aspects, and assets protection
- Pacific utilization
- Selecting and promoting productive actions that support the user chain vision

- Capacity to develop the region and space where the end users apply their objects or services (technical, economical, and environmental issues)
- Regulatory compliance (Legal, Export/Import)

The User Chain, at last, increases the capacity to explain the complete cycle, until new unmet requirements and redefinition of needs occur. It also allows greater integration among those who produce and those who use by defining roles and identifying issues which were insofar without clearly assigned responsible parties for matters such as sustainability, recycling, and disposal. This new perspective involves the buyer in all parts of the complete value chain.

The value chain starts with the end user. Information and requirements are loaded upstream onto the various tiers of suppliers, developing into rights and duties of use, so as to guarantee suitability, sustainability, and responsibility. USER CHAIN (or userchain) means placing the user as the first and last link in the chain. All other participants in the cycle become consequences of the existence of the user, which is the one who uses, purchases, and pays.

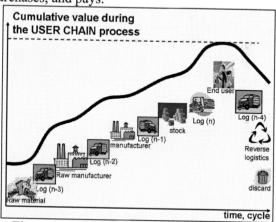

Figure 54 – Value for each step: Schematics

The end user can be identified comparing the added values throughout the entire cycle. The highest value is reached at the end user phase, when such receives and applies the object or service received from the previous chain.

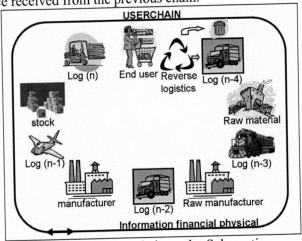

Figure 55 – User chain cycle: Schematics

The figure above shows the sequence starting on the user demand and flowing to the first step of the cycle.

The cycle is a loop, as it starts with the end user demand and ends with the end user recycle or disposal of the goods.

Each step has in turn a supplier and an end user. An interface exists for each step and specifications, scope, time, quality, conditions, and demand; the information must be discussed by each of the agents depending on the type of demand prevalent in the user chain.

There are two basic types of demand:

- Firm: starts with a clear quantity of a product.
- Probable: starts with a forecasting and an anticipated production, making the product available but without sales commitment.

The first scenario is frequent in huge and exclusives investments, without different application options. (Customized specifications, low-frequency projects, etc.)

The second scenario is common for general specifications, multiple users, and the open and competitive market. (High quantity consumption, retail, etc.)

For the first scenario the risk is the cost of shortages, halting a production line by the unavailability of some resource.

For the second scenario the risk is the out of stock, the creation of a competing alternative for the end user.

There are further ways to classify demand, depending on various frequency characteristics:

- Spot demands: very low frequency and without probable future occurrences.
- Continuous demand: linear, stable, growing or decreasing, but with a good forecasting capacity.
- Cyclical and seasonal demands: limited forecasting.
- Random demand: no forecasting, usually with probability of shortages and out of stock instances.

Furthermore, based on the type of the end user demand there are functions and procedures for the previous processes that are productive steps that come before the final consumption. Beyond the value chain, there are information gains to be realized in the user chain methodology. Today's demand chains, independently of their characteristics (Spot, Continuous, etc.) limit the quality of information received from the previous link in the chain. Some information can be lost at each resulting interface. The consequence: distortions in the perception of the demand, over-stocks in increasing trends and shortages in decreasing periods, all with their cumulative taxation on the final price and resources consumed by the chain.

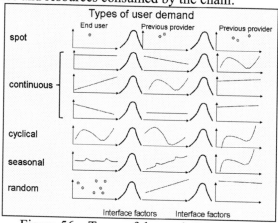

Figure 56 – Types of demand: Schematics

The uncertainty of each step and the risky vision for the entire process give the end user the clear capacity to define and influence strategies, choosing the best alternative available. Each interface can be treated with quantitative models and using standard deviation to measure and smooth out variations and establish controls.

The following picture shows a sequence of a productive process and the quantitative variables considered in an end user demand system.

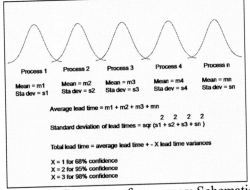

Figure 57 – Sequence of processes: Schematics

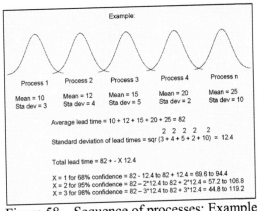

Figure 58 – Sequence of processes: Example

Based on the desired level of confidence, a range can be offered to the end user by explaining that fluctuations are part of the reality and reduced variations mean high costs. Some strategic choices can be done based on the impact on the main productive processes and the cost destined to reduce such impacts. In the example given above depending on the confidence percentage desired, higher confidence means wider lead-time windows. The resulting differences between the Supply Chain and the User Chain are shown in the following table, which closes this chapter.

Supply Chain	User Chain
The market prospects needs.	Users explain their needs and demands based on use
Those who produce establish the specifications.	Users intervene in the project's specifications.
Those who produce are responsible.	Users are co-responsible for requirements based on use.
There is no explicit responsibility over the certification of the life cycle.	Users certify the life cycle of a product.
There is no specification about how post-use return will be treated.	An obsolete product is returned by the user and collected by the producer.
The responsibility for discard and collection is spread out.	Users are responsible for disposal and producers for collection.
Innovations are the supplier's responsibility only, by prospective market analysis.	Users co-share the responsibility for innovations.
Environmental responsibilities are spread out.	Users are co-responsible for environmental issues.
Cost advantages are suppliers' priority. Under pressure of market competition, suppliers pass them on.	Cost benefits are passed on to users.
The issue of sub-suppliers is poorly defined, except for business and supply guarantees.	Responsibility for sub-suppliers is co-shared by the main supplier and users.

* Thanks to Ricardo Ortiz and Rodrigo Cavanha for their comments in this charpter

18 - Negotiation Times in Intensive Assets

Companies with intensive assets focus largely on the values of goods, services, undertakings and inputs, since all these parcels represent a high percentage of the total value employed. For example, in an integrated petroleum company (oil + gas), as in similar other asset intensive enterprises, the business takes on specific characteristics along the productive chain. These characteristics require distinct treatments and adjusted operating profiles, from the process of finding hydrocarbons to the process of distribution of derivatives to the market (Figure 59).

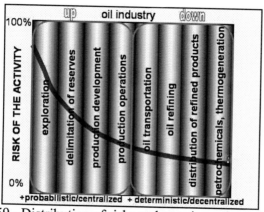

Figure 59 - Distribution of risks and premiums throughout the petroleum process

At the point where the operation starts, upstream, large risks coexist and at the same time, large premiums. In this phase, the activity tends to be more dynamic and the control variables time, coordination of resources, and competence focused on temporal results have priority. Knowledge, concepts and resources are shared with partners who sometimes are also competitors. The style of organization tends to concentrate on few groups or in just one group of excellence, creating synergy of knowledge and successive critiques of content. Because it is a nomadic phase, it ideally has little or no decentralization.

Further downstream, where lower risks and lower premiums are common, other variables become relevant, like work on scale, economies of costs, resource sharing. Ultimately, all these variables aim at using the assets efficiently and inexpensively throughout a sustained amount of time.

These particular characteristics do not demerit any of the phases of an integrated petroleum company or of an asset intensive company. They only differentiate them and require a deeper understanding of the worries and attitudes of each group that comprises the company. Such an understanding is necessary because the rationale behind these characteristics and the ways to reach business satisfaction are quite distinct. Not that these variables are captive to each phase (upstream or downstream). I mean, upstream processes also require scale and low costs, efficiency and sharing (Figure 60). However, short response times and focused competence are more relevant in this phase (upstream) because of the nature of the activity. On the other hand, time and focused competence are also important variables downstream.

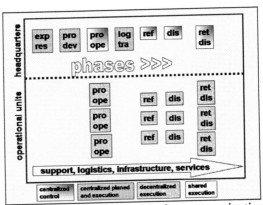

Figure 60 – Risk-based petroleum organization

The UPSTREAM phase, therefore, requires different strategies compared to the DOWNSTREAM one, not because of tradition or the personal taste of leaders of petroleum companies, but because the demands, worries and profitability depend on these different issues, emphases, and ways of doing things. Ideally, once all the essential variables of each phase are achieved, the other variables may be sought too. Then, even larger gains can be pursued without losses or loss of focus on the essential variables of each phase, which are synonymous with survival.

There are petroleum companies that distinguish the two phases so markedly that they tend to separate the operations for upstream and downstream, making them totally independent. Others are more interested in optimizing the sum of the parts, even if each of the component parts does not obtain maximum results when operating in isolation.

19 – Risk and Uncertainty: Real and unpredictable environments

Nature does not follow the rational models that humankind studies; actually, it hardly recognizes them. Sequences of facts have their own law of formation and inexorable application.

Non-predictable events, known as chance, are the results of coinciding random independent time series. Since there is no other way to study the theme except by the generation and analysis of models, we can select two factors which coexist in these relationships with real environments: Risk and Uncertainty.

By drawing on Newendorp (1975), risk may be classified as the probability or chance of a determined event occurring, and uncertainty as the size or dimension of the fact, in case this happens. In other words, risk only correlates with the possibility of an event occurring, independently of its magnitude. Uncertainty correlates with the magnitude of this event, in case it happens. For example, an earthquake in China has a 10% risk of happening in the next 10 years. Uncertainty relates to the magnitude of this earthquake in case it happens or how intense it can be.

Thus, Risk is expressed in percentages or probability ratios of something happening.   Uncertainty is expressed by the magnitude of the event, whether it is an incident, an accident, a disaster, a catastrophe, if we only take events of unfavorable nature as examples. The evaluation of uncertainties' magnitude is subjective. Some renowned authors provide empirical scales that serve as references for distinct events of the same kind.

When failure occurs, people may have ambiguous perceptions of it, since various factors may have caused it. For example, they may attribute failure to successive risks that have gone unforeseen; or yet to an error in the evaluation of chances of occurrence for a given phenomena; or even to "bad luck" (a normal result of Risk). In addition, people perceive loss largely differently when both Risk and Uncertainty apply equally to other environmental operators, or when they see Risk and

Uncertainty applying to only one environmental operator. If Risk is common among all operators, the level of commitment and dedication tends to increase; daring reaches higher limits compared to situations in which there is perception of isolated individual risks only.

Further exploring this idea, Blasius (1976) states that if it becomes known that the process does not occur randomly, but according to defined rules and laws, then there is the possibility of controlling the system or making predictions for its course or one of a similar process. If the variations and conditions of the process are within limits that may be associated to laws and rules, then we are dealing with extrapolatory prediction material.

Bergamini (in Cavanha, 1994) adds that "because we are incapable of controlling chance, we resort to what is within our reach: We try to evaluate the probability of occurrence of a given fact. We fill our language with contingency words: generally, probably, maybe..."

This, however, does not eliminate the necessity to improve techniques, deepen theories, run pilot systems or simulate hypotheses. To the contrary, it stimulates thinking, the capacities to do preventive work, understand, disseminate good practices, and elevate the well being of all involved.

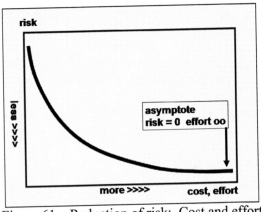

Figure 61 – Reduction of risk: Cost and effort

For each risk variable there is a relation between cost or effort and reduction of the risk, as Figure 61 illustrates. Effort to attain risk zero tends toward infinity in probabilistic environments. The combination of the various variables brings to light the vision of the complete, complex system, that has only a probable solution. One common way of reducing the impacts of undesired phenomena, fruits of the activity's risks, is by sharing the operations with others. This does not necessarily mean that a reduction will be attained.

In Logistics, risk factors are present from the understanding of the marketing parameters to the imponderable constraints of transportation, without forgetting market movements and client satisfaction. There is not, in Logistics, any action that does not require an understanding of its associated Risk and previously planned contingency options. Logistics could be well placed in the field of material probabilities.

20 –Questions for further study

To further encourage you to pursue studies in the area and motivate debate of ideas, below I suggest a series of topics that might illuminate your journey.

1-Supply chain in asset intensive industries

Describe which forms take the supply chain in asset intensive industries (asset intensive industries are understood as those in which the value of the assets has a significant importance for the whole of the organization. They entail purchases, services, undertakings and specific assets such as goods, products and so on).

How should agreements with allied partners or suppliers be negotiated?

How to select and negotiate partnership agreements with similar operators (in the same business field)?

How to evaluate alliances?

What should a contingency plan be like (for terminating a partnership)?

How to break alliances?

How to be a partner and competitor at the same time, in separate projects, with similar companies?

How to form operational committees to act in partnerships? Who should participate?

2-Logistics Alliances: Prepare and validate criteria for selection of partners

List the main parameters that guide the selection of partners.

Which reasons should direct these choices?

Which logistics activities are the most interesting for partnerships?

How to strategically stay tuned to the activities outside the partnership?

How many partners should we have for each activity?

What should be written in a partnership agreement?

3-Logistics organization in companies

How should logistics be positioned in the organization?

Discuss shared services and logistics. Are there differences?

Which are the main activities of logistics in production and transportation companies?

What is the level of representation of a logistics manager?

At which level should he be positioned at the administrative level?

Where does Logistics suitably position itself in an Organization? Why? Consider its participation in the strategy of the company x support. Consider also Logistics as a strategy and/or as support.

Discuss Logistics in functional and processual visions.

Discuss the regional optimization in Logistics, for companies with many business units.

Third parties or direct employees: which logistics should be third partied?

4-Identification of logistics trade-offs: consider each trade-off and their characteristics

Which are the main logistics trade-offs?

How to quantify trade-offs?

How to reduce the false dilemmas of vision 0 or 1 (or 8 / 80) in the organization? The radical visions?

When and how useful are trade-offs ?

When and how should trade-offs be treated and attenuated?

5-Benchmarking in Logistics: How to contract, how to evaluate

How to do benchmarking?

How to contract a consultant?

How much is a consultant worth?

What to monitor in the work?

How to present the results?

How to lever actions as a result of the diagnosis?

How to absorb knowledge and retain competence after benchmarking?

What steps follow an important diagnosis?

6-Cost of shortages: Quantification

Quantify the cost of shortages in production and on the market, from the logistics viewpoint.

What frequency is acceptable for shortages? What frequency is acceptable for lack of resources and components for production? Or for lack of finished products on the market?

In which situations are shortages allowed? How to predict and manage shortages?

Consider responsibility for shortages and collections: What is the logistics situation? What is its role?

Consider shortages and their corrections: What is the cost? What is the cost of preventing shortages? How much is it worth?

When do shortages really matter or is it only a hypothesis?

How to deal with shortages probabilistically?

7-Logistics "variance:" How to measure logistics gain

What is the gain brought by Logistics?

How to discriminate between logistics gains and production, or marketing ones?

How to quantify the gains brought by Logistics?

How to maintain and monitor acceptable levels that had been conquered?

How to expose the logistics gains without creating internal conflicts in the organization?

How much would one pay for third party logistics?

8- Logistics "capacitance:" How to absorb logistics variations?

How to deal with the unexpected in demand logistics?

How to deal with demanding systems with excessive variation?

How to size teams in non-laminated logistics?

How to negotiate possible unexpected variations with production and sales?

How much does it cost to absorb variations?

9-Cost of logistics errors: Modeling

How much do logistics errors cost?

How many and what were the errors in the last 12 months in your company?
How to show clients the logistics errors? Can this attitude lever alliances or is it a humiliation?
How to ensure that future errors will not occur? Does the word guarantee exist in this environment?
When the error is not Logistics, how to deal with and forward the theme internally? What about externally?

<u>10-Logistics strategies for small companies: Main characteristics and sharing</u>
Should small companies have logistics systems similarly to large ones?
Should they contract? What? Third parties?
Should they share with external providers? When? How?
What costs in logistics would be acceptable for small companies?

<u>11-Acquisition by life cycle: Cost x price</u>
How to assemble total cost spreadsheets to support decisions about cost of use for the cycle instead of only prices?
How to share this information with users and suppliers?
How to approach the market by showing the internal cycle of use? Should this be considered improper sharing of confidential data?
How to pay for the life cycle? Discuss possible penalties and bonuses for the suppliers.
Compare the following scenarios: Contract a function x to buy equipment and operate (for example: contract reception of cubic feet of fluid instead of buying pumps and managing operators+maintenance+spare parts).
Compare rental x purchase. When to use one and the other? Think of cases. What variables should be taken into account?

<u>12-Posponements and production risks and gains</u>
How to evaluate the elasticity of risks and gains?
When is postponement appropriate?
Who decides this?

When does postponement become frequent or cascade down the chain?

How to control interlaced activities and postponement?

13-Logistics Interfaces; Logistics and the Productive Chain; Logistics and Marketing: connections, dependencies and service agreements

What are the main logistics interfaces in the organization?

How to format the interface-oriented relationships?

How to quantify losses of interfaces?

How to dilute interfaces?

What is the difference between a true interface x one artificially created to simulate a value?

What are the processes of each activity (production, logistics, and marketing) and how to set up the interfaces between the various actors?

21 – Logistics / Procurement differences between the US and Brazil, from a Petrobras perspective

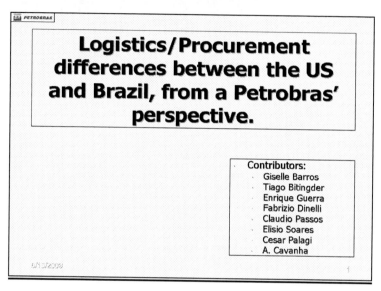

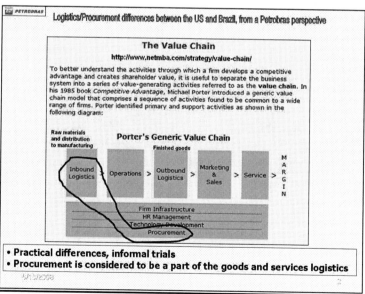

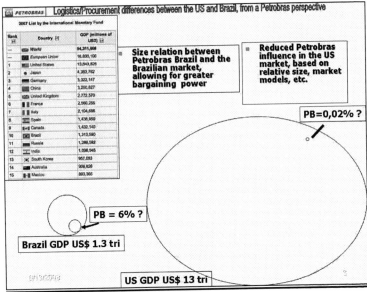

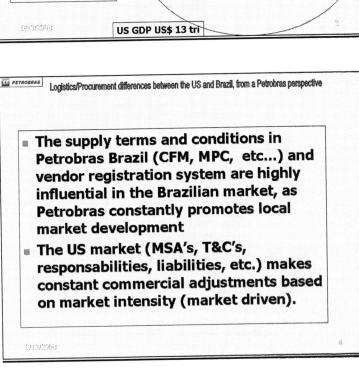

PETROBRAS

Logistics/Procurement differences between the US and Brazil, from a Petrobras perspective

- **The absence of additional oil operators in Brazil and as Petrobras has so many different prospects, makes Petrobras a sole contractor of goods and services for the industry;**

- **US Oil Agencies limit partnerships for bidding processes that produce more than 1.8 million bbl/day.**

PETROBRAS

Logistics/Procurement differences between the US and Brazil, from a Petrobras perspective

- **Petrobras buyers in Brazil are better prepared in technical specifications matters when compared to US buyers, in general.**

- **It is likely a result of the constant transferring of operational personnel to procurement and contracting in Petrobras Brazil.**

- **The US however, regarding the market, is better prepared in procurement acquisitions and tactics procedures (Supply chain, TCO, MSA, BO, DA, etc);**

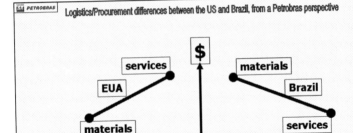

PETROBRAS Logistics/Procurement differences between the US and Brazil, from a Petrobras perspective

- In the US, *materials* have a low cost and *services* are of high cost;
  - Materials: series production, many consumers, high production
  - Services: labor is expensive, employability level is high, growth in qualified local personnel (US born)
- In Brazil, **materials** are expensive and **services** of low cost;
  - Materials: low consumption, not many consumers
  - Services: labor is highly available, investments fluctuate

---

PETROBRAS Logistics/Procurement differences between the US and Brazil, from a Petrobras perspective

- Purchases in the Petrobras Brazilian market contain far more formalizations ("red tape"), as per legislation (law 8666, dec 2745, etc.), as it is a partialy state owned company, for its existance in a still developing market and possible consequences for suppliers in bid loses with Petrobras.
- US norms and regulations are passed by strong and distinguished entities, with constant and intense participation from privately owned operators. The State and public organizations are practically those who pass legislation based on scenarios presented by the operators, self protecting themselves, by creating norms to push away from them operational risks.

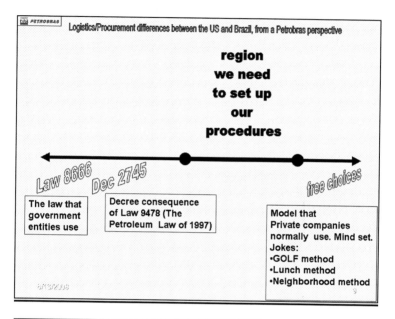

PETROBRAS
Logistics/Procurement differences between the US and Brazil, from a Petrobras perspective

region
we need
to set up
our
procedures

Law 8666   Dec 2745   free choices

The law that
government
entities use

Decree consequence
of Law 9478 (The
Petroleum Law of 1997)

Model that
Private companies
normally use. Mind set.
Jokes:
•GOLF method
•Lunch method
•Neighborhood method

PETROBRAS
Logistics/Procurement differences between the US and Brazil, from a Petrobras perspective

- **Many foreign companies have already established branches and offices in Brazil, due to the many opportunities Petrobras offers its newcomers, once these operate with TRANSPARENCY and EQUAL OPPORTUNITY, even through constant national efforts to always have local participation in projects.**

- **Not all hold stocks in Brazil, support, post-sale assistance, manufacturing facilities (as they prefer a representation method instead) nor do they always produce the best results for the country, although provided with ease of negotiation and language assistance.**

- **Contracts in Brazil are in part supported by a civil code, which defines some of the common commercial relations.**

- **As per in the US, it is a common practice that most the terms and conditions are written in order to have validity.**

- **In the US, MSA's (Master Service Agreements) are used to establish the general Terms and Conditions prior to commencement of work, between two companies, a supplier and client, in order to prepare for any future business opportunity which may come.**

- **MSA's do not posses a time nor a value CAP (As they are "evergreen" contracts); the purchase or service orders are complementary to the contract, adding scope and value.**

PETROBRAS Logistics/Procurement differences between the US and Brazil, from a Petrobras perspective

- **There is a structured penalties mechanism in Petrobras Brazil;**
- **In the US, this is substituted by a group of clauses such as liquidated damages, indemnity, termination... These allow for their enforcement as they are truly needed, excluding loss of profits, and help in perserving a good relationship with suppliers.**

PETROBRAS Logistics/Procurement differences between the US and Brazil, from a Petrobras perspective

- **Petrobras in Brazil uses a pre-qualification system as it has historically been the country's main industry developer and continious investor in the Brazilian Oil market.**
- **In the US market, its own dynamics regulate its existance and quality, acting as almost a self-qualifier; this applies to operators (business uncertainties, probabilistic environment) and first tier goods and services suppliers;**
- **On the other hand, suppliers' sub-contractors (firm demand, deterministic environment), go through a demanding pre-qualification.**

See next slide>>>

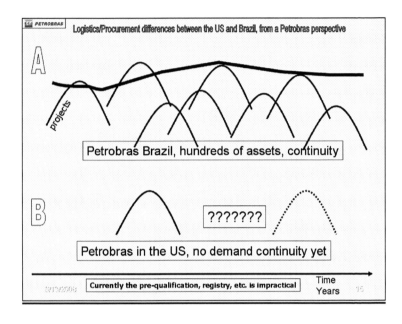

In Brazil, **shared resources** partnerships, through service vendors, have been rarely diffused; in comparison to the partnerships amogsts oil operators (competitors yet partners at the same time)

- In the US, when a supplier fails to succeed in a tender (bid), it moves on to other clients
- In Brazil, when the same occurs, supplier moves onto another industry

PETROBRAS   Logistics/Procurement differences between the US and Brazil, from a Petrobras perspective

- In the US, discount requests must be somewhat justified, in Brazil "barganing" is culturaly well accepted.
- In the US, discounts are offered by the seller, due to high technology rotation and short product life cycle (obsolescence);
- Note: The above may change, be the opposite, depending on commercial enviroment and or industry

PETROBRAS   Logistics/Procurement differences between the US and Brazil, from a Petrobras perspective

- In the US:
  - The number of stages or levels of approval for contracts or purchases is lower; as they are normally harnessed to pre-existing contracts such as "blanket order", MSA's, etc.
  - New vendor selection is subject to high executive level negotiations within a company's business organizations.
- In Petrobras Brazil, new vendor selection at high executive level is only approved, not selected.

Logistics/Procurement differences between the US and Brazil, from a Petrobras perspective

In Petrobras Brazil:
- ### The publishing of bids and their results is a common and expected practice from the public and supplier groups

In the US:
- ### The same level of public or corporate commitment does not exists in regards to bid results.

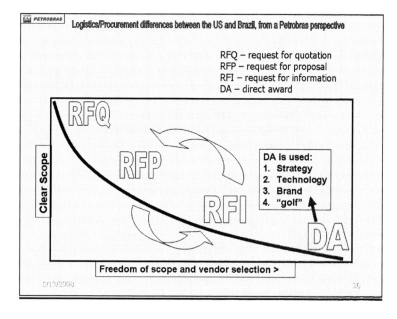

Logistics/Procurement differences between the US and Brazil, from a Petrobras perspective

RFQ – request for quotation
RFP – request for proposal
RFI – request for information
DA – direct award

DA is used:
1. Strategy
2. Technology
3. Brand
4. "golf"

Clear Scope

Freedom of scope and vendor selection >

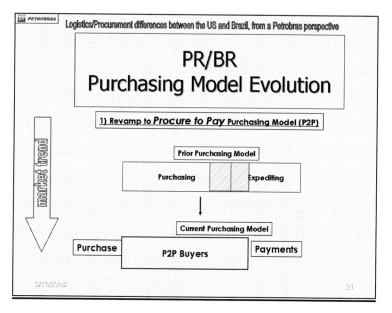

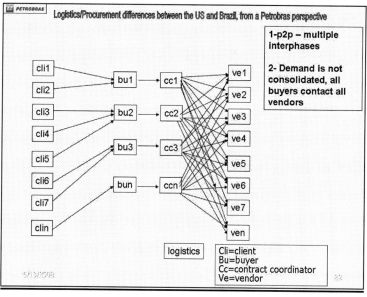

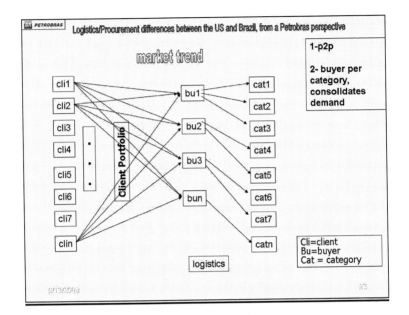

In the US:
• Strong standards for logistics (pick-up, transportation, storage, delivery) due to volume and repetition;
• Logistics norms are product of economic analysis;
• There is strong predisposition to add similarities (final destiny, dimentions, weight, type...) for continuous operational demands;
• Strong predisposition to budget for specific projects, due to the existance of diverse logistics operators specilized in projects only, others only focused on disaster, recovery, etc.

See next slide >>>

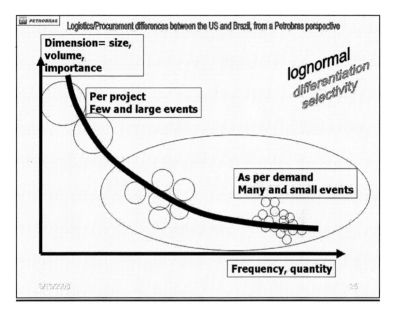

PETROBRAS — Logistics/Procurement differences between the US and Brazil, from a Petrobras perspective

•In the US:
  •The repetition and the systematization make everything run <u>by the book</u>;
  •The acceptance of exceptions make is a difficulty for the mental model of mass production; the American market has difficulties in implementing solutions, it only uses what it has available and standardized; <u>if something is not available, it is not implemented (refused);</u>
  •<u>Rules first, second adaptability;</u>

Logistics/Procurement differences between the US and Brazil, from a Petrobras perspective

"In Brazil, the top 500 companies spend R$ 39 billion annually in logistics activities. Despite this significant effort, in countries like the US and Japan, 25% of all companies have a logistics department, or outsource this service; in Brazil, this figure does not exceed 2%, which proves the room for improvement for these activities."

(From an interview with a professor from the UFRJ)

Logistics/Procurement differences between the US and Brazil, from a Petrobras perspective

- Do not confuse best practices with best theories;
- Verify if reality "the ideal" is being implemented.

Logistics/Procurement differences between the US and Brazil, from a Petrobras perspective

MAKE IT SIMPLE
KEEP IT SIMPLE

thanks
cavanha@petrobras.com.br

* Thanks to Carlos Huerta for his comments in this charpter

Selected Readings

BACHELARD, G. (1984). *A Filosofia do Não*. Lisbon Portugal: Editora Presença. [The philosophy of no: A philosophy of the new scientific mind. New York, NY: Vicking Press, 1968].

BACHELARD, G. (1968). *O novo espírito Científico*. Rio de Janeiro, RJ: Biblioteca Tempo Universitário. [The new scientific spirit, Boston, MA: Beacon Press, 1986].

BANFIELD, Emiko. (1999). *Harnessing value in the supply chain: Srategic sourcing in action*. Hoboken, NJ: John Wiley & Sons.

BLANCHARD, B.S. (1992). *Logistics, Engineering, and Management*. Upper Saddle River, NJ: Prentice Hall.

BOWERSOX, D.J., CLOSS, D.J. (1996). *Logistics management: The integrated supply chain process*. Columbus, OH: MacGraw Hill.

CAVANHA, A.O. (1994). *A totalidade biológica e o desenvolvimento harmonioso* [The biological totality and the harmonious development] . Curitiba, PA, Brasil: Universidade Federal do Paraná (UFPR).

CAVANHA FILHO, A.O. (2000). *Simulador logístico para o custo da falta* [Logistics simulator for the cost of shortage]. Florianópolis, SC: Universidade Federal de Santa Catarina, Brazil (UFSC).

DISNEY, S.M. (1997). Dynamic simulation modelling for learning logistics. *International Journal of Physical Distribution & Logistics Management*, *27* (3/4), p. 174.

NEWENDORP, P. D. (1975). Decision Analysis for Petroleum Exploration. Tulsa, OK: Pennwell Publishing Company.

PECHT, Michael. (1995). The Product Reliability, Maintainability, and Supportability Handbook. New York, NT: CRC Press.

PORTER, M. E. (1990). *Vantagem competitiva: Criando e sustentando um desempenho superior*. Brazil: Editora Campus.[Competitive advantage: Creating and sustaining a superior performance. New York, NY: Free Press. A division of MacMillan].

SCHECHTER, Chris. (1998). *Characterization of the cost of forecast error in a complex supply chain.* Digital Semiconductor Engineering Department.

SCHULZ, R. (1999). One percent error rate = 10 percent of logistics' cost. *Material Handling Engineering*, August, p. 93-97.